The Ultimate Wildlife Habitat Garden

The Ultimate

WILDLIFE HABITAT GARDEN

Attract and Support
Birds, Bees, and Butterflies

STACY TORNIO

Timber Press
Portland, Oregon

Published in 2024 by Timber Press, Inc.,
a subsidiary of Workman Publishing Co., Inc.,
a subsidiary of Hachette Book Group, Inc.
Hachette Book Group
1290 Avenue of the Americas
New York, NY 10104

timberpress.com

Printed in China on responsibly sourced paper

Text design by Sarah Crumb
Cover design by Hillary Caudle
Illustrations by Jenna Lechner

Front cover (clockwise from top left): Aster by Dreamstime/Pixelarchitect, indigo bunting
by Dreamstime/Paul Sparks, milkweed by Dreamstime/Skorpionik00, common buckeye by
Dreamstime/Lthomas57
Back cover (clockwise from top left): Yarrow by Dreamstime/Baker244, garden illustration,
cosmos by Dreamstime/Tatyanaego, Anna's hummingbird by Dreamstime/Fallsview

The publisher is not responsible for websites (or their content) that are not owned by
the publisher.

The Hachette Speakers Bureau provides a wide range of authors for speaking events. To find
out more, go to hachettespeakersbureau.com or email HachetteSpeakers@hbgusa.com.

ISBN 978-1-64326-142-3
Catalog records for this book are available from
the Library of Congress and the British Library.

CONTENTS

I WANT TO ATTRACT
BIRDS
13

I WANT TO BRING IN
BUTTERFLIES
131

I WANT TO WELCOME
OTHER WILDLIFE
169

I WANT TO ATTRACT
HUMMINGBIRDS
67

I WANT TO GARDEN FOR
BEES
97

SHOW ME HOW TO
PLAN A GARDEN
187

FAQS
208

PREFACE

When I started working at *Birds & Blooms* magazine more than fifteen years ago, I found myself reconnecting with a pastime that had always been part of my life—gardening. Long before I called myself a gardener, I was digging in the dirt; sowing seeds; and growing veggies, flowers, trees, and shrubs. My mom has dozens of pictures of me in the garden. My brother and I even had our own veggie stand at the local farmers' market when we were kids. Good ol' Ada, Oklahoma, had an epic market back in the day.

It wasn't just veggies, either. Everyone in my family and extended family gardened, and we grew everything imaginable. There always seemed to be something in bloom, and in turn, there was always something to see when I was outside. Hummingbirds zipped around, birds frequently nested in our backyard, and bees and butterflies visited the flowers.

I didn't realize that this was unique or special until I started working at *Birds & Blooms*. The magazine was filled with beautiful reader stories that reminded me of my childhood, and there seemed to be even more people who wanted to know how to achieve similar success. I hadn't done much gardening after I went to college and moved away from Oklahoma, but every issue of the magazine had me dreaming of plants I'd like to grow in my own garden—someday. When I settled into my first real home, I knew I wanted to bring life into my yard, just as my parents, grandparents, and other relatives had been doing for years.

I started off small and ordered a predesigned garden plan (plants included) from a mail-order company called Bluestone Perennials. Over time, I enhanced that simple original layout and then expanded into other areas of my yard as I tried to do my part to make a wildlife-friendly space.

I spent about ten years at the magazine. I learned from and worked with some of the best gardening experts in the industry. As editor, I had the honor of passing on their wisdom to more than one million subscribers who were also dedicated to creating a better space for birds, hummingbirds, bees, butterflies, and other wildlife.

Over the years, many friends have asked me for gardening advice or plant recommendations. I love introducing them to a plant (like my go-to favorite, the purple coneflower) and then telling them it can attract wildlife, as well. I call this approach "Plants with Purpose," because there are so many plants that do more than look pretty: they support animals, wildlife, and a strong ecosystem.

This book isn't about what I think about plants or what I know about gardening. It's more a culmination of what I've learned from the many great gardeners in my life. I hope it helps you discover some of the wonderful Plants with Purpose that will bring birds, bees, and other wildlife into your garden. They need all the help they can get. Thank you for doing your part through the power of gardening.

INTRODUCTION

If you picked up this book, you probably already know the importance of gardening for wildlife. You likely know about the threats to birds, bees, and butterflies caused by the ongoing loss of the habitats they rely on. So let's skip the statistics, agree that we have an opportunity to help pollinators do their essential work, and provide beauty, joy, and vitality through our efforts as gardeners who seek to harness the power of plants.

Without a doubt, a thriving, plant-filled yard is more attractive to birds, bees, butterflies, and other pollinators and wildlife. Best of all, when you intentionally grow for one of these groups, there's a good chance you'll support the others, because, as you'll read in this book, many plants offer benefits for three, four, or five different groups of wildlife. I call this a "Birds & Bees" approach to gardening, because when you focus on the birds and the bees you'll naturally attract others. Many of the plants in this book are perfect for mixing and matching. See something you love in the humming-bird chapter? It's probably also ideal for bees. Love the look of a shrub you see in the bee chapter? It'll also make good cover for butterflies. Using the Birds & Bees approach isn't that difficult; it just helps you decide what to look for, in order to maximize your space.

My goal is to help you learn about the wildlife you can attract to your yard, create a vision, and then put it into motion—season by season and plant by plant. You might start small by switching to organic gardening practices or by reading plant descriptions and labels in seed catalogs and at the garden center to find a bee-friendly flower. All of these efforts make a difference, for you and the environment.

While the book is organized by chapters, everything in here is intended to be layered together, to help you create a vibrant and attractive garden. Start with a strong base and then build as you go. It won't be long before you'll see a lot more life in your garden. It all starts with the birds and the bees.

I Want to Attract BIRDS

Birds make backyards better—and front yards, patios, decks, and porches. Even windowsills. When I go outside to garden or relax, there's something really special about seeing a bird perched or flying nearby. I feel good knowing my garden helps support the birds in my area.

I've learned that by selecting plants with bird-friendly benefits, I can attract dozens of species throughout the year. You can, too. Yet, gardening on its own can get you only so far. To truly create a bird haven, you should plan for a few other things. Here are some of the best ways to bring birds into your yard, now and in the future.

According to the U.S. Fish and Wildlife Service, about one-third of households in the United States feed wild birds at some time during the year.

FEED BIRDS WELL

Offering food is one of the easiest things you can do to bring birds into your yard, and thanks to the hobby of bird feeding, it's also one of the quickest. Here's a look at the different types of feeders you can buy and what you might expect to attract with each one.

Tray feeder

A tray feeder can accommodate larger birds because it's often a big, open area. This type of feeder usually is mounted on a post or is placed on the ground or other flat surface. You can use pretty much any seed with these feeders, including the popular black oil sunflower seeds and seed mixes. Keep in mind that squirrels often will use these feeders, too—and they'll eat a lot of seed.

Hopper feeder

This is probably the most common and popular backyard feeder, and it comes in a wide range of shapes and sizes. Most models are available to hang from a hook, branch, or pole; some have a baffle or weighted mechanism to prevent squirrels from accessing the seeds. You can use black oil sunflower seeds or seed mixes.

Tube feeder

Tube feeders are some of the most popular types of bird feeders. Most dispense thistle seeds, although some tube feeders also will hold seed mixes or hulled sunflower seeds. These feeders often have weighted mechanisms or baffles to keep squirrels out.

Suet feeder

The most common type of suet feeder is a hanging cage into which you put an entire square "cake." Other types of suet feeders include hoppers that hold multiple cakes, or logs that contain suet in predrilled holes.

Peanut feeder

These feeders usually come in a tube or circular shape with large holes that allow birds to dig out individual whole or shelled peanuts.

Sugar-water feeder

You can find sugar-water feeders specifically designed for orioles and hummingbirds. Oriole feeders are often orange while hummingbird feeders are usually red. Both hold a sugar-water mixture and likely include multiple perches.

Other feeders

Other feeder types include those that hold orange halves or other fruit, which appeal to orioles and sometimes tanagers, and mealworm feeders, which can attract bluebirds, robins, or wrens. If you have questions about the best kinds of feeder(s) for your situation, visit a farm-supply business or a local store that specializes in bird feeding and/or gardening. You might also reach out to a local Audubon Society or nature center. Not only will you get great tips, but you'll support your community.

PROVIDE WATER, IF POSSIBLE

Birds, bees, butterflies, and other beneficial insects and wildlife need clean water, whether for bathing, drinking, or breeding. While only certain types of birds will visit a bird feeder, most species will appreciate your birdbath.

Of the three main elements—food, water, and shelter—required for certification by the National Wildlife Federation's Certified Wildlife Habitat program (www.nwf.org/garden-for-wildlife), providing adequate clean water for drinking and bathing is often the most challenging for home gardeners. It doesn't have to be.

If you're not fortunate enough to have a free-flowing stream or pond on your property, add a simple birdbath to start. If you want to take it up a notch, consider a fountain or water feature. Moving water can make a big difference in catching a bird's attention. If you have a birdbath or water feature with deep sections, try adding small rocks to give birds an extra place to perch.

All of these require some regular maintenance. Your pollinator friends need clean, fresh water to avoid waterborne illnesses, so scrub your

> The best plants offer a triple dietary benefit—seeds, nectar, and berries. Often, these will be shrubs or trees.

> Look for solar devices to go into your birdbath, either to heat the water or circulate the water through a fountain. These make your bath more appealing to birds and help prevent the growth of algae.

water source frequently with nontoxic cleaners. Refill it with fresh water. Keep it ice-free if you live in an area where it dips below freezing in winter.

CREATE AS MUCH NATURAL SHELTER AND HABITAT AS POSSIBLE

Shelter and habitat are critical for birds, especially because we lose so many wild and natural places each year. It can feel daunting to create a bird-friendly habitat, especially if you're starting from scratch. But with every annual, perennial, shrub, and tree you plant, and every water source you supply, you're helping create a strong future for birds, bees, and other wildlife.

While you're planning this habitat, try to make it as diverse as possible. This means including plants that produce nectar, berries, and seeds. When you select a new plant from the seed catalog or garden center, ensure that it will benefit birds. Many—but not all—will. By making this a rule, you'll be doing so much good for the birds that visit your yard. When planning the perfect habitat, this is a case where more often is better. Birds tend to like spending time in and nesting in dense areas where they are protected. You can create this environment by being mindful of layering. If you plant a shrub or two in one spot, go ahead and make an entire garden bed out of this area by placing perennials in the front and leaving room for hooks to support hanging baskets and feeders on the sides. Slowly but surely, you'll start to fill out an area that will appeal to the birds.

PLAN FOR ALL FOUR SEASONS

By planning for birds that might visit your yard in any season, and providing food or nectar, shelter, and/or nesting sites, you'll maximize the number of avian visitors you attract and help wildlife in general. Offer foods that resident and migrating birds prefer at different times of the year. Select plants that will support wildlife continuously.

Evergreens provide four-season appeal in your yard. Not only will you enjoy their rich green foliage and shade, but they'll provide good shelter for birds.

KEEP YOUR YARD FREE OF PESTICIDES

You're planning a bird-friendly yard. You might not realize it, but most commercial fertilizers, soil treatments, and weed sprays actually hurt or kill birds and pollute soils and water, so please make a conscious effort to reduce or eliminate the use of synthetic pesticides and herbicides. This will help keep birds, bees, butterflies, and other wildlife healthy.

FILL YOUR GARDEN WITH NATIVES

As you select plants for your yard, understand that natives are most likely to benefit birds. To find the species best suited to your location, contact a native plant society in your area; your local nursery, gardening, or nature organization; or the extension service run by your state university. Many of these groups offer lists of native plants and regular plant sales. They'll help you get started and support you as you develop your garden.

A big reason native plants are so good for birds is because they naturally attract the local insects some birds require.

Discover Common Bird Species

As you plan your garden, it's helpful to be familiar with some of the common bird species that are most likely to show up in your backyard. AllAboutBirds .org is a great online resource that provides maps and regional information. Remember that males can look different from females or juveniles, so if you don't recognize a bird right away, don't give up. It might just take a little more digging to figure out what you're seeing.

These are some of the easiest birds to attract with a bird feeder. Invest in a good thistle feeder, and they'll visit your backyard throughout the year.

American goldfinch
Spinus tristis

American goldfinches are such welcome sights in backyards across North America. You can easily spot their bright yellow feathers during breeding season. In winter or early spring, you might have to look for other identifying marks, like their black wings, in order to recognize them.

LENGTH Up to 5.1 inches

WINGSPAN Up to 8.7 inches

FEMALE MARKINGS Dull olive-yellow body, distinctive black-and-white wings

MALE MARKINGS Bright yellow during breeding season (similar to a canary); dull yellow-brown the rest of the year

SOUNDS Resembles "po-ta-to-chip" and "per-chick-o-ree"

HABITAT Overgrown and weedy areas, parks, backyards

NESTING Shrubs or small trees in fairly open areas

DIET Mostly seeds, some insects

RANGE Most of the United States during some portion of the year; year-round throughout much of the middle latitudes of the United States

American robin
Turdus migratorius

The American robin is one of the most recognized and common birds in North America. Many people think of the robin as a sign of spring, but it's actually found year-round throughout most of the United States; you just don't see it as often in winter. The robin often nests in backyards, so you might be fortunate and get an up-close look at the nesting process.

LENGTH Up to 11 inches

WINGSPAN Up to 15.8 inches

FEMALE MARKINGS Orange breast, gray wings and head; white on lower belly is hard to see

MALE MARKINGS Same as female but heads can be slightly darker

SOUNDS Spring song "cheerily, cheer up, cheer up, cheerily, cheer up"

HABITAT Woodlands, backyards, parks

NESTING Trees, nesting platforms, other odd spots like lighting fixtures

DIET Worms, insects, fruit

RANGE Most of North America

If you put a nesting platform in a well-protected tree, you may attract these backyard favorites.

All orioles are easy to attract to backyards with oranges and sugar water. If you don't live in the Baltimore oriole's range, look for other orioles like the Bullock's, orchard, and hooded.

Baltimore oriole
Icterus galbula

Bring bright and beautiful orioles to your backyard with a sugar-water oriole feeder, orange halves, and the right plants. These birds show up like clockwork every year in spring, ready to build their nests and raise a family. If you time it right, you can attract them when they arrive and then enjoy them all season.

LENGTH Up to 7.5 inches
WINGSPAN Up to 11.8 inches
FEMALE MARKINGS Light orange to olive from head to underside; long, pointed bill

MALE MARKINGS Bright orange underneath, vibrant black head and back, pointed bill
SOUNDS Single and varied notes and a familiar "chuck" sound
HABITAT Open areas, edges of woods, near rivers
NESTING Woven basket suspended from the fork of a branch of a deciduous tree
DIET Insects, fruit, nectar
RANGE Throughout much of the eastern and mid-western United States

Chickadees in North America have similar habits and patterns. Depending on where you live, also look for the Carolina, mountain, boreal, and chestnut-backed.

Blue jays love acorns, so they often hang out in oak trees. They've even helped "plant" lots of oaks while foraging.

Black-capped Chickadee

Poecile atricapillus

Chickadees are some of the most friendly and common backyard birds in North America, and you can easily attract them year-round by stocking your feeders with seeds and suet. Combine this with a birdhouse and plants that provide food and shelter, and you're well on your way to creating a chickadee haven.

LENGTH Up to 5.9 inches

WINGSPAN Up to 8.3 inches

FEMALE MARKINGS White band on head, black cap, gray overall on top, lighter undersides

MALE MARKINGS Same as female

SOUNDS Well-known call sounds like "chick-a-dee-dee-dee"; another song resembles "fee-bee"

HABITAT Forests, woods, parks

NESTING Old woodpecker holes or tree cavities; birdhouses

DIET Seeds, insects, berries

RANGE Year-round in northern United States and southern Canada

Blue jay

Cyanocitta cristata

Blue jays are big, beautiful, and loud. You can easily attract them with most seeds, and they especially love peanuts. Like their relatives in the crow family, they are intelligent and verbal, so they can be fun to watch. If you have mature trees and shrubs, they might choose to nest in your yard.

LENGTH Up to 11.8 inches

WINGSPAN Up to 16.9 inches

FEMALE MARKINGS Blue-and-white body, distinctive head crest, black stripe around head, white wing bars

MALE MARKINGS Same as female

SOUNDS Soft songs to jarring cries; most known for loud "jeer" or "jay-jay"

HABITAT Forests, parks, backyards

NESTING Branches about 10 to 20 feet above the ground

DIET Omnivorous: primarily nuts, seeds, berries, fruit

RANGE Year-round throughout the eastern United States; parts of the west in colder months

Cedar waxwing
Bombycilla cedrorum

Cedar waxwings are some of the most beautiful and active nomads among birds, moving from one area to the next to feed on fruit and berries. They travel in large groups—from dozens to even hundreds of birds. You may also spot their cousins, Bohemian waxwings, in these flocks. The two species look very similar and their ranges overlap.

LENGTH Up to 6.7 inches

WINGSPAN Up to 11.8 inches

FEMALE MARKINGS Brown head and crest, black eye mask, cream/yellow underparts, gray on top, distinctive yellow tip on tail, red band on wing tips

MALE MARKINGS Same as female

SOUNDS Thin, high-pitched lisp that sounds like "bzeee"

HABITAT Open woodlands, orchards, yards, especially near water

NESTING Horizontal branches and forks in trees from 3 to 50 feet tall; often in colonies

DIET Fruit, berries, insects

RANGE Throughout the United States and southern Canada

Plant lots of fruit-bearing trees or shrubs in your yard to attract large groups of waxwings.

Dark-eyed juncos are common backyard feeder birds. They'll eat sunflower seeds but prefer millet.

Dark-eyed junco
Junco hyemalis

For many Americans, the appearance of dark-eyed juncos is one of the first signs that colder weather is coming. They often hang out on the ground below feeders, foraging for seeds. Plant shrubs to give them plenty of cover.

LENGTH Up to 6.3 inches

WINGSPAN Up to 9.8 inches

FEMALE MARKINGS Usually slate-gray with white outer tail feathers

MALE MARKINGS Same as female but with regional color variations

SOUNDS Various songs, including warbles and whistles

HABITAT Forests, wooded areas

NESTING Often on the ground, but also on low branches or building ledges

DIET Seeds, insects

RANGE Seasonally throughout North America

It's fun to look for the red mark on the back of this bird's head to determine if it's a male or female.

Downy woodpecker
Dryobates pubescens

This is the most common woodpecker in backyards across the United States. If you have one or more feeders, there's a good chance you'll see a downy. It'll stop for seeds, suet, fruit, and even a little nectar from sugar-water feeders. If you see or hear this bird drilling on wood, it's probably looking for insects.

Downy woodpeckers and their cousins, hairy woodpeckers, are small backyard birds that look very similar but appear in slightly different areas. It's fun to try to get both of them to your backyard, and to try to identify their differences.

LENGTH Up to 6.7 inches

WINGSPAN Up to 11.8 inches

FEMALE MARKINGS Black-and-white stripes on lower body and wings, bolder black-and-white bands on head and neck

MALE MARKINGS Same as female, but with red cap on back of head

SOUNDS Quiet "pik"

HABITAT Wide variety, including woodlands, parks, backyards

NESTING Cavities in dead trees and limbs

DIET Mostly insects but also seeds, berries, acorns, suet

RANGE Throughout North America except the Southwest and northern Canada

Eastern bluebird

Sialia sialis

Watch for eastern bluebirds' flashy blue colors near open fields in spring and summer. That's where they find abundant insects to sustain them while visiting and nesting. They really like mealworms, especially when they're nesting, so consider putting a mealworm feeder in your backyard. If possible, keep the feeder in the shade for the benefit of both the birds and the worms.

LENGTH Up to 8.3 inches

WINGSPAN Up to 12.6 inches

FEMALE MARKINGS Orange-brown breast, grayish above, hints of blue in wings

MALE MARKINGS Blue above, rusty throat and underside

SOUNDS Short, warbling song; call sounds like "tu-a-wee"

HABITAT Grassland

NESTING Cavities in birdhouses or old woodpecker holes

DIET Mostly insects; some fruit, berries

RANGE Eastern United States, with many staying year-round

If you have an open, grassy area like a field, park, or farm near your backyard, consider putting up a bluebird nesting box. Be sure to research the proper shape, materials, and dimensions before you buy or build one, and install it correctly. Also, ensure that it has a predator guard to keep the bluebirds safe.

Eastern towhees are so similar to spotted towhees, which are found in the western United States, that they were considered the same species until recently.

Eastern towhee

Pipilo erythrophthalmus

What is that large bird scurrying around your yard or pecking around the bottom of your feeders? It might be a towhee, looking for food or a place to build a nest. This bird loves shrubs, brush, and wild areas. It gives you a good reason to add shrubs to your backyard design.

LENGTH Up to 8.2 inches

WINGSPAN Up to 11 inches

FEMALE MARKINGS Brown head and back, rufous underside

MALE MARKINGS Rufous-and-white underside; black back, tail, head, throat, wings

SOUNDS "Drink-your-tea" or "to-wheee"

HABITAT Overgrown fields, woodlands

NESTING Often in the ground but sometimes in a shrub up to 4 feet tall

DIET Insects, seeds, fruit

RANGE Eastern United States

Evening grosbeak
Coccothraustes vespertinus

The evening grosbeak is a favorite in winter because it often arrives at feeders when other birds have left for the season. This large bird frequently flies in groups, so if you see one, you'll likely see many more. They'll stop by for a wide range of seeds and berries.

LENGTH Up to 7.1 inches

WINGSPAN Up to 14.2 inches

FEMALE MARKINGS Gray body, black-and-white wings, hints of yellow on neck

MALE MARKINGS Yellow-black-and-white body, yellow stripe over eye

SOUNDS Sometimes a short warble

HABITAT Forests, especially with conifers

NESTING Usually high in conifers

DIET Seeds, berries, insects

RANGE Throughout much of North America

Evening grosbeaks can be unpredictable; they go wherever food and weather take them. Sometimes you'll see dozens in a weekend and then none for years.

Gray catbird
Dumetella carolinensis

Catbirds are common during spring and summer, so you might see them traveling through your yard, or going to and from their nests. They can be elusive, hiding deep in shrubs and thickets in parks and along roadsides. They have beautiful coloring, and it's fun to look for their rusty underside.

LENGTH Up to 9.4 inches

WINGSPAN Up to 11.8 inches

FEMALE MARKINGS Slate gray body, black cap and tail; rusty underside can be hard to see

MALE MARKINGS Same as female

SOUNDS Short notes and phrases strung together; mimics other birds

HABITAT Shrubs, thickets, forests

NESTING Branches of shrubs, trees

DIET Insects, fruit

RANGE Throughout North America except the far West

Catbirds are true mimics. They've been known to produce more than 100 sounds, including the meowing of a cat.

Curious about how to tell the difference between a hairy and a downy woodpecker? It's tricky. They look a lot alike, but the hairy is up to three inches longer, with a more pronounced bill.

Hairy woodpecker
Dryobates villosus

If you have a dead tree or limb, don't take it down. Instead, leave it up for hairy and downy woodpeckers; they may find bugs and insects, and even carve out a nest in the decaying wood. The hairy woodpecker is less common than the downy. You can attract both with suet and seeds.

LENGTH Up to 10.2 inches

WINGSPAN Up to 16.1 inches

FEMALE MARKINGS Black-and-white back, white belly, bold black-and-white stripes on head

MALE MARKINGS Same as female but with red cap on head

SOUNDS Similar to, but louder than, downy's "pik"

HABITAT Woodlands, parks, backyards, especially with large trees

NESTING Cavities in dead trees and limbs

DIET Primarily insects; also berries, seeds, acorns, suet

RANGE Throughout much of the United States and southern half of Canada

House finches often travel in large groups, eating and foraging together. If one house finch stops at your feeder, get ready to replenish your seed because you'll likely see more.

House wren
Troglodytes aedon

House wrens may look plain and brown, but these common backyard visitors are fun to watch, especially during breeding season. They work tirelessly to gather materials for the nests they build just about anywhere, even in less-than-ideal places. Both males and females cock their heads a bit as they perch. Other wrens to look for in North America include Bewick's, cactus, canyon, sedge, and winter.

LENGTH Up to 5.1 inches

WINGSPAN Up to 5.9 inches

FEMALE MARKINGS Brown and tan overall; short, erect tail with subtle black-and-white stripes; thin bill

MALE MARKINGS Same as female

SOUNDS Males: long, musical songs during mating season; both males and females chatter and squeak

HABITAT Most habitats with trees and shrubs, including parks and yards

NESTING Old woodpecker holes, nest boxes

DIET Insects

RANGE Throughout the northern two-thirds of the United States and southern Canada during nesting season; Central and South America in winter

House finch
Haemorhous mexicanus

House finches are common visitors to backyard feeders. You can attract them easily with black oil sunflower seed. They'll stay in the same area throughout the year, so you may be able to observe them for months.

LENGTH Up to 5.5 inches

WINGSPAN Up to 9.8 inches

FEMALE MARKINGS Brown overall, streaked belly

MALE MARKINGS Similar to female but with red chest, throat, face

SOUNDS Warbling notes ending in "zeee"; also "cheeps"

HABITAT Wide range includes backyards, parks, forests

NESTING Trees, other birds' nests, ledges

DIET Seeds, berries, buds and flower parts, some insects

RANGE Common year-round in both the eastern and western United States

The best way to bring wrens into your yard is to put up a nest box with the right dimensions. These birds also are known to nest in unusual spots, like on top of a mailbox or in flowerpots and shoes.

Indigo buntings will stop at thistle feeders. You also might be able to bring them to your yard by offering mealworms.

Lazuli bunting
Passerina amoena

The lazuli bunting is like the western counterpart of the indigo bunting. This beautiful blue-hued bird is a bright spot in spring and summer. By planting shrubs like serviceberry or elderberry, you might even attract it to nest in your backyard.

LENGTH Up to 5.9 inches
WINGSPAN Up to 8.7 inches
FEMALE MARKINGS Light cinnamon brown
MALE MARKINGS Vibrant blue head, blue wing spots, orange tinges on breast, strong white wing bar
SOUNDS Repeated squeaky notes
HABITAT Brushy, wooded areas near streams
NESTING Shrubs, low trees just 3 feet above the ground
DIET Insects, seeds, berries
RANGE Western United States during breeding season

You can attract the lazuli bunting to feeders with one of its favorite snacks: millet. It also will stop for sunflower or thistle seeds.

Indigo bunting
Passerina cyanea

The indigo bunting is the bluest and one of the most vibrantly colored birds. Look for it during spring migration, in your backyard, nearby parks, or wildlife areas. By planting shrubs, you'll create a safe and welcoming space for this striking bird.

LENGTH Up to 5.1 inches
WINGSPAN Up to 8.7 inches
FEMALE MARKINGS Brownish body, some streaks on breast
MALE MARKINGS Bright blue overall, especially on head
SOUNDS Up to 200 songs per hour
HABITAT Brushy and weedy areas, especially edge habitats
NESTING Shrubs, low trees at edges of forests
DIET Seeds, insects, berries
RANGE Eastern United States during breeding season

Meadowlarks aren't typical backyard visitors, but they may appear if you live near grassy, open areas. You'll increase your chances of seeing them if you grow native plants and use organic methods because you'll attract the insects they feed on.

Eastern and western meadowlarks

Sturnella magna (eastern) and *Sturnella neglecta* (western)

These two birds look so similar many people think they're the same species. The best way to tell them apart is their songs. You'll often see meadowlarks sitting on fence posts in summer, singing or looking for their next insect meal.

LENGTH Up to 10 inches
WINGSPAN Up to 15.8 inches
FEMALE MARKINGS Black-tan-brown-and-white stripes on back; yellow underneath with distinctive black bib

MALE MARKINGS Same as female
SOUNDS Eastern: whistles resembling "tee-yah, tee-yair"; Western: gurgling, flute-like song of 7-10 notes
HABITAT Grasslands, prairies
NESTING Woven nest on the ground in open fields
DIET Mostly insects, some seeds
RANGE Eastern common in the eastern United States; Western common in the West

Mourning dove
Zenaida macroura

The mourning dove is one of the most common and beautiful backyard birds in North America, even though it doesn't get a lot of attention. With just a little effort, you might attract groups of mourning doves to eat, nest, and just hang out. Most of this bird's diet consists of seeds, and it often feeds on the ground under feeders or plants.

LENGTH Up to 13.4 inches

WINGSPAN Up to 17.7 inches

FEMALE MARKINGS Gray-and-brown body, black spots on the back

MALE MARKINGS Same as female

SOUNDS Distinctive, soft "coo-oo"

HABITAT Trees, semi-open woodlands, grasslands, farms, parks, deserts

NESTING Dense foliage, on the ground, or on building ledges

DIET Seeds

RANGE Year-round throughout the United States and Mexico, breeding from southern Canada into Mexico

The cardinal is the state bird of seven states: Illinois, Indiana, Kentucky, North Carolina, Ohio, Virginia, and West Virginia.

Northern cardinal
Cardinalis cardinalis

The northern cardinal is one of the most popular backyard birds. If you live in the eastern United States, it's fairly easy to attract it to your backyard with seeds and feeders. Male and female cardinals often travel together and mate for life, so it's fun to look for couples stopping by your yard.

LENGTH Up to 9.1 inches

WINGSPAN Up to 12.2 inches

FEMALE MARKINGS Pale brown overall, hints of red in crest and wings, bright red beak

MALE MARKINGS Bright red body and beak, black mask and throat

SOUNDS Songs resemble "birdie, birdie, birdie"

HABITAT Forests, thickets, backyards

NESTING Up to 15 feet above the ground in dense shrubs or trees

DIET Seeds, insects, berries, fruit

RANGE Year-round throughout the eastern United States

The soft, hooting calls of a mourning dove might trick you into thinking there's an owl nearby.

You can attract northern flickers to your yard with nest boxes, a birdbath, or suet.

Northern flicker
Colaptes auratus

If there's a northern flicker in your backyard, you'll probably know it. Not only is it a large bird, but its striking coloration, call, and flight are easily identifiable. This bird might not eat from your feeders, but you'll see and hear it hammering on trees and poles while it hunts for insects. Attract flickers like you would other woodpeckers.

LENGTH Up to 12.2 inches

WINGSPAN Up to 20.1 inches

FEMALE MARKINGS Spotted cream-and-black belly, striped brown-and-black back, broad black bib, gray and brown areas on head and neck, red streak extending from beak, red patches on back of head and underside of tail

MALE MARKINGS Similar to female but with a black mustache

SOUNDS Rolling rattle, "kyeer"

HABITAT Woodlands, forests, semi-open areas

NESTING Cavities in dead trees, limbs

DIET Ants and other insects, fruit, berries, some seeds and nuts

RANGE Throughout North America, except northernmost Canada

While mockingbirds aren't typically feeder birds, they still pass through backyards frequently. If you live in their wintering grounds, you might see them eating berries during colder months.

Northern mockingbird
Mimus polyglottos

Is that a frog you heard, or a mockingbird? This bird will imitate just about any sound in nature, including frogs, toads, and other birds. The mockingbird is one of the largest birds you're likely to find in your backyard. To verify that you're looking at one, check for white flashes in its wings while it's flying.

LENGTH Up to 10.2 inches
WINGSPAN Up to 13.8 inches

FEMALE MARKINGS Gray-brown overall, white wing bars visible in flight
MALE MARKINGS Same as female
SOUNDS Series of phrases that make up a song; also mimics other birds and animals
HABITAT Backyards, parks, forests
NESTING Branches of trees, shrubs
DIET Insects in summer; berries and fruit in winter
RANGE Year-round in the lower half of the United States; northern areas during nesting season

Pine siskin
Spinus pinus

These birds often travel in flocks and are a bit nomadic. You might see them in your backyard one week and not again for a long time. They feed on a wide range of plants and sometimes will stop at your feeders for seeds and suet.

LENGTH Up to 5.5 inches

WINGSPAN Up to 8.7 inches

FEMALE MARKINGS Brown-and-cream streaks all over, hints of yellow on wings and tail

MALE MARKINGS Same as female

SOUNDS Whispery songs; call note sounds like a watch being wound

HABITAT Forests, parks, suburbs

NESTING Branches far out on conifers

DIET Seeds, flower parts, insects

RANGE Throughout North America

Purple finches use their large bills to crack open seed hulls or flowers to get at the seeds and nectar.

Pine siskins can store seeds in their esophagus (called the crop) to eat later. This is especially handy during cold winters.

Purple finch
Haemorhous purpureus

Purple finches and house finches appear similar at first glance, but if you look more closely, you'll see that the purple finches have a deeper, more purple coloring, especially on the head. Purple finches are less common than house finches, so consider yourself lucky if you see this one in your backyard.

LENGTH Up to 6.3 inches

WINGSPAN Up to 10.2 inches

FEMALE MARKINGS Brown-and-white streaks

MALE MARKINGS Reddish-purple breast, wings, head

SOUNDS Warbling song; "tek" sound in flight

HABITAT Forests, wooded streams, tree-filled backyards

NESTING Limbs in mature trees

DIET Seeds from trees, weeds, grasses; tree buds; flowers; insects; berries; small fruit

RANGE Eastern United States

Purple Martin
Progne subis

Look for large groups of purple martins during nesting season; you might be fortunate to see flocks of hundreds or even thousands of birds as they prepare to migrate to wintering grounds in South America. You can attract them to your yard with birdhouses, especially if you live near open fields that provide an endless supply of insects.

LENGTH Up to 7.9 inches
WINGSPAN Up to 16.1 inches
FEMALE MARKINGS Dull blue-gray overall
MALE MARKINGS Bright, iridescent blue-purple overall; black-brown wings and tail
SOUNDS Males: normal song a bit croaky; "hee-hee" sound when fighting over territory. Females: "choo" when calling to fledglings
HABITAT Open fields, especially near streams, wetlands, dunes, deserts
NESTING Primarily man-made structures, especially multi-roomed birdhouses and gourds; also natural cavities, including old woodpecker holes
DIET Insects
RANGE Eastern United States and south-central Canada during nesting season

Red-bellied woodpecker
Melanerpes carolinus

The red-bellied woodpecker's name is confusing to many people because you can't easily see the red belly. If you can see it from the right angle, you might spot the tinge of red at the far edge of the belly, near the tail. You can't miss the bold red stripe that runs from the top of its bill to the nape of its neck and its distinctive white-and-black striped back and wings. The red-bellied is a frequent backyard visitor.

LENGTH Up to 9.4 inches
WINGSPAN Up to 16.5 inches
FEMALE MARKINGS Black-and-white pattern on the back, pale belly, red on the back of the head
MALE MARKINGS Similar to females but red extends from the back of the head to the front bill
SOUNDS Descending, sometimes repeated "kwirr" or "churr"
HABITAT Deciduous woodlands, orchards, yards, parks, especially near water
NESTING Cavities in dead trees, limbs, fence posts
DIET Insects, nuts, seeds, fruit
RANGE Eastern United States

To attract these birds to your backyard, put out suet, black oil sunflower seeds, and peanuts. They've even been spotted at hummingbird feeders.

It's common to see red-winged blackbirds at your feeder. They enjoy a mix of seeds in a tray or hopper feeder and also forage on the ground beneath feeders.

Red-winged blackbird

Agelaius phoeniceus

If you've ever been to a marsh, you've probably seen (and heard) a red-winged blackbird. This is one of the earliest birds to arrive and start nesting in spring. It prefers to nest in swampy areas, where it feeds on a plethora of insects.

LENGTH Up to 9.1 inches

WINGSPAN Up to 15.8 inches

FEMALE MARKINGS Streaked brown with hints of yellow around the bill

MALE MARKINGS Jet black with bold red-and-yellow wing bars

SOUNDS Musical "conk-la-ree"

HABITAT Marshes, hayfields

NESTING Low in shrubs or vegetation

DIET Insects, seeds

RANGE Throughout North America

Attract rose-breasted grosbeaks to your feeder with sunflower or safflower seeds. They'll also stop by for peanuts.

Scarlet tanager
Piranga olivacea

The scarlet tanager is gorgeous, with bright red feathers that rival the cardinal's. It's not a regular backyard visitor, but this one might stop by for fruit. If you're lucky, it might choose to nest in your yard. It loves berries, so plant shrubs that produce fruit, especially in summer and through early fall.

LENGTH Up to 6.7 inches

WINGSPAN Up to 11.4 inches

FEMALE MARKINGS Olive-yellow body; darker wings, tail

MALE MARKINGS Bright red body; black wings, tail

SOUNDS Distinctive "chick-burr" (Some people say they sound like a hoarse robin.)

HABITAT Forests, open areas, gardens

NESTING Shrubs, tree branches usually distanced from the tree's trunk

DIET Insects, fruit

RANGE Eastern United States during nesting season

Rose-breasted grosbeak
Pheucticus ludovicianus

The male rose-breasted grosbeak almost looks as if it's been painted. You'll love seeing this bird at your feeders in spring, along with humming-birds and orioles. All grosbeaks have large, distinctive bills.

LENGTH Up to 8.3 inches

WINGSPAN Up to 13 inches

FEMALE MARKINGS Brown-and-cream streaks, white eyebrow

MALE MARKINGS Black on top, white underneath, bright red breast patch

SOUNDS Whistling song similar to American robin

HABITAT Forests, thickets, orchards

NESTING Often in forked branches of young trees

DIET Insects, seeds, berries, fruit

RANGE Eastern United States during breeding season

If you want to increase your chances of seeing this bird, keep an eye out during its spring and fall migrations.

Owls often sit very still, which makes it hard to spot them even when they're nearby. To increase your chances of seeing them, start looking around dusk, when they tend to be more active.

Screech owl

Eastern: *Megascops asio;* Western: *Megascops kennicottii*

Although eastern and western screen owls are found in different parts of the country, they're quite similar in appearance, habitat, and diet. You might not think of owls as typical backyard birds, but many screech owls do visit, and hunt and live in inhabited areas. They're the most common owls you might see on your property. You can increase your chances of attracting them by installing a nest box. Screech owls are the only owls that are likely to use a nest box.

● ● ● ● ● ● ● ● ◗

LENGTH Up to 9.8 inches
WINGSPAN Up to 24.4 inches

FEMALE MARKINGS Gray-black-white-and-cream streaks all over; ear tufts (An adult red morph variety, more common in the northern United States, has copper coloring and streaking.)
MALE MARKINGS Same as female
SOUNDS Eastern: whinny, wail, purr, trill; western: series of hoots
HABITAT Forested areas, suburban areas with dead snags
NESTING Tree cavities, old woodpecker holes, nest boxes
DIET Varied, but primarily insects, small mammals
RANGE Eastern: common in the eastern half of the United States; western: concentrated in the West

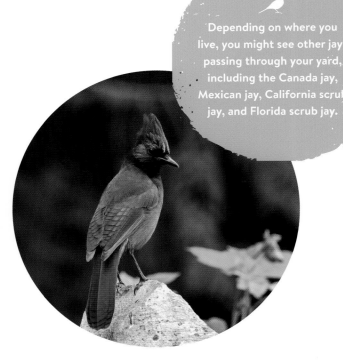

Depending on where you live, you might see other jays passing through your yard, including the Canada jay, Mexican jay, California scrub jay, and Florida scrub jay.

Steller's jay
Cyanocitta stelleri

Steller's jays bring their bright colors, curiosity, and daring to your yard. They're a lot of fun to watch. Like the blue jays, Steller's jays often will stop at your backyard for seeds and peanuts. In summer and fall, they gather and store these foods for colder months.

LENGTH Up to 13.4 inches
WINGSPAN Up to 17.3 inches
FEMALE MARKINGS Bright blue lower half and tail; black head, chest; distinctive crest
MALE MARKINGS Same as female
SOUNDS Loud "shook-shook-shook-shook"
HABITAT Wooded areas, especially with conifers
NESTING Close to trunks of conifers
DIET Omnivorous: primarily insects, seeds, nuts, fruit, small animals
RANGE Western United States

Summer tanager
Piranga rubra

A close cousin of the northern cardinal, the summer tanager is one of the brightest and boldest birds you can bring into your backyard. The best way to attract this bird is by planting berry-producing plants and shrubs, although sometimes it's attracted to hummingbird feeders.

LENGTH Up to 6.7 inches
WINGSPAN Up to 11.5 inches
FEMALE MARKINGS Yellow overall, distinctive bill
MALE MARKINGS Fiery red body, thick bill
SOUNDS "Pit-ti-tuck" and a call similar to the American robin's
HABITAT Parks, gardens, woodlands
NESTING Forks of branches, sometimes among leaves
DIET Insects, fruit
RANGE Lower United States; in the East and West during breeding season

If you see a summer tanager on a perch, take a close look at what it's doing. It's known for catching bees or wasps in flight and then striking them against a branch to kill them.

Look for many other common swallows—like bank, barn, cave, and cliff—catching insects in spring and summer.

Tree swallow
Tachycineta bicolor

You often can identify a tree swallow by how it sits on a wire or swoops low over an open field to capture insects. To bring this bird to your yard, put up a birdhouse (especially one designed for bluebirds) and choose plants that attract its primary food—insects—and other wildlife.

LENGTH Up to 5.9 inches
WINGSPAN Up to 13.8 inches
FEMALE MARKINGS A bit brownish above; some blue, green, and white on underside

MALE MARKINGS Brighter than females with deep blue on top, black tail and wings, black band around eye and chest, white throat and belly
SOUNDS High-pitched chips, twitters
HABITAT Fields, marshes, any areas near water
NESTING Natural cavities, birdhouses
DIET Insects; some berries, mostly in winter
RANGE Throughout most of North America during nesting season; the far south in winter

This bird's favorite feeder snack is black oil sunflower seed. You can also attract it with suet, especially in winter.

Tufted titmouse
Baeolophus bicolor

The tufted titmouse might be tiny and plain-looking, but it's an active, entertaining, and friendly backyard bird found throughout much of the eastern United States. In other regions, you might spot its titmice cousins: oak, bridled, juniper, and black-crested. All of them have a signature crest. You might attract titmice with feeders; birdhouses; nest boxes; and plants that appeal to their primary foods—including insects, spiders, and caterpillars—and also might provide nuts, berries, and small fruit.

LENGTH Up to 6.3 inches

WINGSPAN Up to 10.2 inches

FEMALE MARKINGS Silvery gray top, light underneath, black base of bill, ruddy patch next to wing, distinctive gray crest

MALE MARKINGS Same as female

SOUNDS Repeated "peter-peter-peter"

HABITAT Tall, mostly deciduous, trees in woodlands, orchards, parks

NESTING Tree cavities, nest boxes, birdhouses

DIET Insects, seeds, berries

RANGE Eastern half of the United States

Frequently, the year's first brood of bluebirds will help their parents raise subsequent babies with chores like feeding.

Western tanager
Piranga ludoviciana

If you live in this bird's range, you might spot it in your backyard. The male's brilliant scarlet and gold feathers will dazzle you. In fact, you might have to do a double take because you might think you're looking at a canary.

LENGTH Up to 7.5 inches
WINGSPAN Up to 11.5 inches
FEMALE MARKINGS Yellow-green body, gray-and-white wing bars, slight red in face
MALE MARKINGS Bright yellow body, scarlet head, strong black-and-white wing bars
SOUNDS Short, raspy
HABITAT Woodlands
NESTING Trees, sometimes facing open areas
DIET Mostly insects, some berries and fruit
RANGE Western United States in summer

While the western tanager isn't a typical feeder bird, you sometimes can attract it as you would orioles, with sugar-water feeders or fresh-cut oranges and other fruit.

Western bluebird
Sialia mexicana

Similar to the eastern bluebird in color and size, the western bluebird actually has a more vibrant blue hue. The ranges of these two bluebirds barely overlap, so it's a fun challenge to find the two species when you're traveling or visiting other parts of the country. Watch for them swooping through the air like swallows to catch insects.

LENGTH Up to 7.5 inches
WINGSPAN Up to 13.4 inches
FEMALE MARKINGS Gray underside, blue hints in wings
MALE MARKINGS Bright blue across wings, on head, and under throat; red upper breast; white lower breast
SOUNDS Distinctive "kew"
HABITAT Open areas, woodlands
NESTING Old cavities of trees, bluebird nest boxes
DIET Mostly insects; berries and seeds in winter
RANGE Western parts of the United States; year-round in some areas

White-breasted nuthatch

Sitta carolinensis

You'll know you're looking at a nuthatch just by its behavior. It will often be upside down, moving upward from the base of a tree, looking for seeds and insects. While the white-breasted is the most frequently seen nuthatch in North America, you also might spy the red-breasted, pygmy, or brown-headed, depending on where you live.

LENGTH Up to 5.5 inches

WINGSPAN Up to 10.6 inches

FEMALE MARKINGS White underneath, gray above, gray cap on head

MALE MARKINGS Similar to females but with black cap on head

SOUNDS Rapid "wha-wha-wha"

HABITAT Mature trees, woodland edges

NESTING Tree cavities, old woodpecker holes, sometimes birdhouses

DIET Insects, seeds, nuts

RANGE Throughout United States, except southern-most areas

Attract nuthatches with black oil sunflower seeds or suet. They might choose to nest in a small birdhouse.

White-throated sparrow

Zonotrichia albicollis

Don't clear all the brush piles in your yard, because birds like white-throated sparrows really appreciate them. They might even use them for nesting. These birds are common sights as they head north to Canada to nest.

LENGTH Up to 7.1 inches

WINGSPAN Up to 9.1 inches

FEMALE MARKINGS Tan-and-brown stripes, long tail

MALE MARKINGS Body similar to female, but with black-and-white stripes on head and distinctive yellow spot in front of the eye

SOUNDS Whistle resembles "oh-sweet-canada-canada"

HABITAT Forests, tree-lined areas

NESTING Often just above the ground or under trees or shrubs

DIET Seeds, insects, fruit

RANGE Much of the eastern United States; also along the West Coast

White-throated sparrows will stop at feeders for millet and black oil sunflower seeds.

Wood thrush

Hylocichla mustelina

The wood thrush is a close cousin of the American robin. It hangs out on the ground, scavenging for insects among leaves and other debris. Look for the spots on its breast that distinguish it from a robin.

Wood thrushes probably won't show up at your feeder, but they might appear in your backyard. They're shy of humans, but if you learn their songs, you might hear them even if you don't see them.

LENGTH Up to 8.3 inches

WINGSPAN Up to 13.4 inches

FEMALE MARKINGS Reddish-brown above, similar to a robin; spotted pale breast; distinctive white eye ring

MALE MARKINGS Same as female

SOUNDS Resembles "ee-oh-lay"

HABITAT Woods, forests, sometimes backyards

NESTING Dense shrubs, trees

DIET Insects, fruit

RANGE Eastern United States during breeding season

This is one of the few warblers that might appear at feeders for seeds, peanut butter, or suet. The other warbler to look for in backyards is the yellow warbler.

Yellow-rumped warbler
Setophaga coronata

This is one of the most common warblers in North America and the one you're most likely to see in your backyard. Try to spot the yellow rump on its tail. You might see a yellow-rumped warbler in spring but it probably won't stick around long before it heads north to nest in Canada.

LENGTH Up to 5.5 inches
WINGSPAN Up to 9.1 inches
FEMALE MARKINGS Brownish with streaks on breast, yellow patches underneath, yellow on the rump

MALE MARKINGS Similar to females with brighter coloring overall; black mask; bright white throat; vibrant yellow on top of the head, breast, rump
SOUNDS Soft warbles and a call that sounds like "chek"
HABITAT Woodlands, forests
NESTING Branches from 4 to 50 feet high
DIET Insects, berries
RANGE Throughout the United States

Here are some other common birds you might see in your backyard. Plant a diverse and vibrant garden to increase your chances of attracting birds like these.

Black-headed grosbeak

Yellow warbler

Western scrub jay

Red-breasted nuthatch

Chestnut-backed chickadee

Barn swallow

Carolina wren

Red-headed woodpecker

American crow

BIRD PLANT RECOMMENDATIONS

When you plan your garden with birds in mind, you're doing so much good for the environment. Plus, the right plants provide birds with food, habitat, and shelter. Here are some of the plants that are most likely to attract birds to your garden.

The beautyberry does best in warmer climates and sometimes provides fruit for wildlife through winter months.

NATIVE PLANT TIP

Rudbeckia fulgida is native to many parts of the United States. If you want a black-eyed Susan with a bigger native range, look for *Rudbeckia hirta.*

Beautyberry
Callicarpa americana

It's not often that you see bright purple or magenta berries in the wild. The beautyberry is among the few plants that put on such a colorful show. Not only is it stunning, but this shrub provides fruit that birds favor in summer and fall, and it's also relatively disease-free and easy to grow. It's a perfect choice for your wildlife garden.

PLANT TYPE Perennial
HARDINESS Zones 6 to 10
SIZE Up to 6 feet tall and 6 feet wide
FLOWER COLOR Small pink or purple flowers, bright purple or pink berries
SOIL Well-drained soil but tolerates clay
LIGHT NEEDS Full sun to part shade
ATTRACTS Birds

Black-eyed Susan
Rudbeckia fulgida

Most gardeners will find this perennial easy to grow. It's very forgiving; it tolerates a wide range of soils and conditions and will come back bigger and stronger every year. Its seeds are a great food source for birds, and its nectar-filled blooms attract other wildlife. Many gardeners also call it rudbeckia. Some gardeners consider it aggressive, so don't plant it in an area if you don't want it to spread.

> If your black-eyed Susans begin to fade during the summer, cut them back and they might bloom again in fall.

Blue spruce
Picea pungens

Most evergreens will help you attract birds. They provide shelter and nutritious seeds, and their foliage has year-round appeal. Gardeners value the blue spruce because of its attractive silvery-blue color. By adding this to your garden, you can be confident you're supporting a strong bird population for years to come. It's also known as Colorado spruce.

PLANT TYPE Perennial
HARDINESS Zones 2 to 7
SIZE Up to 60 feet tall and 20 feet wide; smaller dwarf varieties available
FLOWER COLOR Nonflowering
SOIL Acidic, well-draining
LIGHT NEEDS Full sun
ATTRACTS Birds

> If you don't have room for a big blue spruce, look for smaller or dwarf varieties like globosa that will reach only five to six feet tall.

PLANT TYPE Perennial
HARDINESS Zones 3 to 9
SIZE Up to 4 feet tall and 3 feet wide
FLOWER COLOR Golden yellow
SOIL Dry to medium well-drained soil
LIGHT NEEDS Full sun to part shade
ATTRACTS Birds, hummingbirds, butterflies, bees

This tree often sends out suckers. Remove them so you don't have little trees sprouting everywhere.

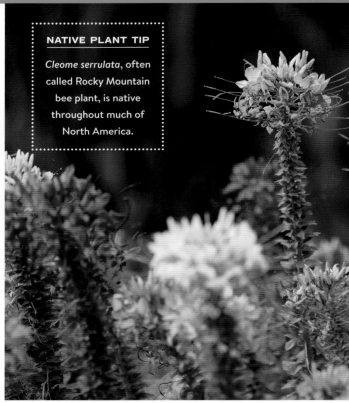

NATIVE PLANT TIP

Cleome serrulata, often called Rocky Mountain bee plant, is native throughout much of North America.

Chokecherry
Prunus virginiana

The chokecherry is a staple tree in bird gardens around the United States. In spring, its showy and fragrant white blooms attract birds and insects looking for nectar. In summer, it offers shelter. Then in late summer and fall, it produces pea-sized berries that darken to purple and black. These make delicious jams and pies, but you may not get the chance to harvest them, since birds and other wildlife may get to them first. Chokecherry also is known as Virginia bird cherry or bitter-berry.

PLANT TYPE Perennial

HARDINESS Zones 2 to 7

SIZE Up to 30 feet tall and 20 feet wide

FLOWER COLOR White

SOIL Well-drained, loamy

LIGHT NEEDS Full sun to part shade

ATTRACTS Birds, hummingbirds, butterflies, bees

Cleome
Cleome hassleriana

Cleomes truly are garden all-stars because of their big, spider-like flowers (hence one of their common names, "spider flower") and because you easily can grow them from seed. More, once you plant them, it'll be a race to see what will get to their seeds first—hummingbirds, other birds, butterflies, or bees.

PLANT TYPE Annual

HARDINESS Annual in most areas

SIZE Up to 6 feet tall and 2 feet wide

FLOWER COLOR Pink, purple, white, bicolor

SOIL Moist, well-drained

LIGHT NEEDS Full sun to part shade

ATTRACTS Birds, hummingbirds, butterflies, bees

This is another perennial you often can get to rebloom in late summer or fall if you cut it back after it first flowers in summer.

These plants often reseed each year: You also can start your own by collecting seeds from the flower heads at the end of the season and transplanting them into your garden in the spring. Why not share seeds with your friends, too?

Coreopsis
Coreopsis lanceolata

If you have challenging soil that is sandy, has lots of clay, or has to endure dry conditions, consider making room for the sunny yellow flowers of coreopsis. It often grows where other flowers won't. Plus, it blooms throughout the summer, comes back year after year, and is a great source of seeds for birds and nectar for hummingbirds and butterflies. Coreopsis also is known as tickseed.

PLANT TYPE Perennial
HARDINESS Zones 4 to 9
SIZE Up to 3 feet tall and 2 feet wide
FLOWER COLOR Generally yellow; newer varieties are red, white, bicolor
SOIL Medium, well-drained
LIGHT NEEDS Full sun
ATTRACTS Birds, hummingbirds, butterflies, bees

NATIVE PLANT TIP

Another coreopsis to look for that is native to North America is *Coreopsis verticillata*, which also is known as threadleaf or whorled coreopsis.

Cornflower is a popular flower in the herb family, and gardeners love it because of its deep, rich color. It is also a popular cut flower because its blooms stay fresh for a long time.

Cosmos
Cosmos bipinnatus

The cosmos, or Mexican aster, is another low-maintenance annual. It is one of the easiest backyard flowers to grow from seed, which makes it a perfect choice for young gardeners. When the flowers appear, they'll attract bees, butterflies, and hummingbirds looking for nectar. Later in the season, birds will stop to eat the seeds. This is another annual that often reseeds itself, so watch for cosmos sprouts next year.

PLANT TYPE Annual
HARDINESS Annual in zones 2 to 11
SIZE Up to 4 feet tall and 3 feet wide
FLOWER COLOR Red, pink, white, yellow
SOIL Average, well-drained
LIGHT NEEDS Full sun
ATTRACTS Birds, hummingbirds, butterflies, bees

Cornflower
Centaurea cyanus

Cornflowers, or bachelor's buttons, are one of those flowers that really seem to do it all. They give off a lot of seeds, so birds love them. Cornflower plants also reseed themselves, even though most gardeners grow them as annuals. Although their blooms aren't big, their bright cobalt flowers and sweet nectar attract hummingbirds, butterflies, and bees.

PLANT TYPE Annual
HARDINESS Annual in zones 2 to 11
SIZE Up to 3 feet tall and 2 feet wide
FLOWER COLOR Blue, purple
SOIL Medium, well-drained
LIGHT NEEDS Full sun to light shade
ATTRACTS Birds, hummingbirds, butterflies, bees

Because cosmos stems can be tall and delicate, plant these flowers close together so they can support each other.

Crabapple

Malus

Crabapple trees often steal the show in spring with their beautiful pink flowers. They're perfect for bees, hummingbirds, and butterflies that need a good nectar source early in the season. Later, they provide ideal nesting sites for birds. Through fall and winter, the berries provide a good source of food for birds like cardinals, waxwings, and robins. Harvest some of the crabapples yourself and make delicious jelly; they're packed with natural pectin so you won't need to add any. Also, plant a crabapple near your apple trees; it'll improve pollination and you'll probably get more apples.

PLANT TYPE Perennial

HARDINESS Zones 4 to 8

SIZE Up to 20 feet tall and wide

FLOWER COLOR Pink

SOIL Well-drained, acidic

LIGHT NEEDS Full sun

ATTRACTS Birds, hummingbirds, butterflies, bees

Looking for the right time to prune your crabapple? Do it in late winter, when it's not actively blooming.

NATIVE PLANT TIP

There are more than 15 different dogwoods native to the United States. Looking for a dogwood native to the West? Try *Cornus nuttallii.*

Another great dogwood to grow for wildlife is red twig dogwood, *Cornus sericea.*

Dogwood
Cornus florida

Every backyard can benefit from a dogwood. Dogwoods' year-round appeal includes blooms in spring, foliage that's green in summer and red in fall, and berries in fall and winter. The botanical name listed here is for flowering dogwood, but there are many other great varieties, which are available as trees and shrubs. Ask for recommendations from your local garden center, extension service, or native plant society.

PLANT TYPE Perennial

HARDINESS Zones 5 to 9

SIZE Up to 30 feet tall and wide

FLOWER COLOR White

SOIL Medium, well-drained

LIGHT NEEDS Full sun to part shade

ATTRACTS Birds, hummingbirds, butterflies, bees

Elderberry
Sambucus canadensis

If you live in a colder region of the country, this is one of the best shrubs you can grow for birds. Look for the plant's tiny white flowers in spring and take a whiff to see if you notice the lemony fragrance. By late summer, the blooms turn into dark purple-blue fruit. You can use berries from elderberry shrubs to make jams, jellies, and even wine, but there's a good chance the birds will get them first.

PLANT TYPE Perennial

HARDINESS Zones 3 to 9

SIZE Up to 12 feet tall and wide

FLOWER COLOR White

SOIL Medium, well-drained

LIGHT NEEDS Full sun to part shade

ATTRACTS Birds, hummingbirds, butterflies, bees

Pair elderberries with other berry-producing shrubs and you'll attract hungry birds for many months.

Feather reed grass
Calamagrostis ×acutiflora 'Karl Foerster'

When you're planning a yard for birds and wildlife, ornamental grasses definitely should be in your mix. Of this grass type, the most well-known among gardeners is the cultivar Karl Foerster, which was named the Perennial Plant of the Year in 2001 by the Perennial Plant Association. Birds love the wheat-like seed heads that appear in late spring and last through fall.

PLANT TYPE Perennial

HARDINESS Zones 5 to 9

SIZE Up to 5 feet tall and 3 feet wide

FLOWER COLOR Not significant but pinkish-purple

SOIL Medium to wet

LIGHT NEEDS Full sun

ATTRACTS Birds

This grass does well under many conditions, including part shade and clay soil, and even is drought-tolerant. Place it behind colorful blooms like purple coneflowers or black-eyed Susans for a strong combo.

Blooming forsythia shrubs make a stunning impact when you group them together. Want to grow more without spending a lot of money? Try taking a stem cutting from an existing plant.

Fountain grass
Pennisetum alopecuroides

Fountain grass is one of the most attractive and easiest grasses to grow, and offers birds food and shelter throughout the year. This grass is perfect in perennial beds and borders, and works well in any other spot in the garden. The foliage is a rich gold in fall that fades to beige in winter.

PLANT TYPE Perennial
HARDINESS Zones 6 to 9
SIZE Up to 5 feet tall and wide
FLOWER COLOR Usually none but sometimes small and silvery-pink
SOIL Medium to wet
LIGHT NEEDS Full sun to part shade
ATTRACTS Birds

If you don't cut these grasses back in the fall, they'll offer birds food and shelter during colder weather.

Forsythia
Forsythia ×intermedia

This shrub's yellow flowers offer one of the earliest and brightest signs of spring, and an ideal source of nectar for early wildlife visitors. Even though the blooms are short-lived, they give way to dense, bright green foliage that's perfect for nesting birds. There are many kinds of forsythia available, so look for the one that works best for you.

PLANT TYPE Perennial
HARDINESS Zones 5 to 8
SIZE Up to 8 feet tall and 6 feet wide
FLOWER COLOR Yellow
SOIL Medium, well-drained
LIGHT NEEDS Full sun to part shade
ATTRACTS Birds, hummingbirds, butterflies, bees

Goldenrod is ideal for wild-flower gardens. In spring, mix some goldenrod seeds with seeds of other flowers and let an area of your yard go "wild."

Goldenrod
Solidago speciosa

Goldenrod flowers aren't big or showy, but they are reliable, drought-resistant, and long-blooming. You often will see this native wildflower in open fields and natural areas from summer to late fall. It survives in a wide range of conditions and is a good, consistent source of nectar and seeds for wildlife. If you have challenging areas in your yard, try goldenrod. It might be the plant that makes it!

PLANT TYPE Perennial

HARDINESS Zones 3 to 8

SIZE Up to 3 feet tall and wide

FLOWER COLOR Yellow

SOIL Average, well-drained

LIGHT NEEDS Full sun

ATTRACTS Birds, hummingbirds, butterflies, bees

Hawthorn leaves turn brilliant colors in fall, ranging from red to orange. You can identify a hawthorn tree by its toothed, triangular leaves and thorny stems.

Hawthorn
Crataegus phaenopyrum

If you have room for only one or two trees in your yard, try a hawthorn. It will give food and shelter to birds. In spring, the clusters of small blossoms will provide nectar for hummingbirds, butterflies, and bees. The blooms transform into bright red berries that feed birds through fall and winter.

● ● ● ● ● ● ● ●

PLANT TYPE Perennial
HARDINESS Zones 3 to 8
SIZE Up to 30 feet tall and wide
FLOWER COLOR White
SOIL Moist, well-drained
LIGHT NEEDS Full sun
ATTRACTS Birds, hummingbirds, butterflies, bees

Joe-pye weed
Eutrochium purpureum

You can often find this perennial growing in swampy areas or alongside rivers or marshes. Its blooms aren't particularly showy, but it thrives in areas that are frequently tough for other plants. It's also an important source of nectar and seeds for wildlife. Consider this a must for any backyard native garden.

NATIVE PLANT TIP

Joe-pye weed is native throughout much of North America. Another variety to look for is *Eutrochium fistulosum*.

The blooms have a slightly vanilla scent. Rub the petals to release the aroma.

PLANT TYPE Perennial

HARDINESS Zones 4 to 9

SIZE Up to 7 feet tall and 4 feet wide

FLOWER COLOR Pinkish red

SOIL Moist, rich

LIGHT NEEDS Full sun to part shade

ATTRACTS Birds, hummingbirds, butterflies, bees

There are more than 40 types of junipers and 400 cultivars, so it's easy to find one in the size, shape, and style that will work best in your yard.

Juniper
Juniperus

This is one of the most versatile evergreens because it's available as both a shrub and a tree. Birds are drawn to junipers' little blue berries and year-round shelter.

PLANT TYPE Perennial

HARDINESS Zones 2 to 9

SIZE Up to 50 feet tall and 30 feet wide

FLOWER COLOR None

SOIL Moist, well-drained

LIGHT NEEDS Full sun

ATTRACTS Birds

Ninebark is named primarily for its continuously peeling bark that ranges from red to brown, tan, and more. This is great for winter interest.

Don't cut purple coneflowers back in fall so birds can feast on the seeds in winter.

Ninebark
Physocarpus opulifolius

Ninebark is a resilient native shrub that can thrive in even the coldest climates, although it sometimes struggles in really hot and humid areas. Between the nectar-rich blooms in spring and fruit in late summer and fall, ninebark is perfect for birds throughout North America.

PLANT TYPE Perennial
HARDINESS Zones 2 to 8
SIZE Up to 8 feet tall and 6 feet wide
FLOWER COLOR White or pink
SOIL Medium, well-drained, slightly acidic
LIGHT NEEDS Full sun to part shade
ATTRACTS Birds, hummingbirds, butterflies, bees

Purple coneflower
Echinacea purpurea

This perennial superstar deserves—and earns—a spot in backyards across the United States. It's drought-tolerant, easy to grow, and has so many wildlife benefits. You'll often see birds, hummingbirds, butterflies, and bees working the pink flowers—all at the same time. As an added plus, when you start with one plant, you'll often have three or four within a few years. Also called echinacea, it's available in several colors.

PLANT TYPE Perennial
HARDINESS Zones 4 to 9
SIZE Up to 4 feet tall and 2 feet wide
FLOWER COLOR Pink
SOIL Medium, well-drained
LIGHT NEEDS Full sun to part shade
ATTRACTS Birds, hummingbirds, butterflies, bees

Like many trees, redbuds don't transplant well. Pick a good spot for them, plant and tend them carefully, and let them thrive.

Redbud

Cercis canadensis

In early spring, sometimes when there's still snow on the ground, the redbud tree will start to bud. Its delicate pink flowers often provide one of the only spots of color in the landscape. It's a welcome sign for early fliers like butterflies, bees, and even hummingbirds that need a good source of nectar. Birds will also eat the blooms or use them in their nests. Later, they'll eat the seeds.

PLANT TYPE Perennial

HARDINESS Zones 4 to 8

SIZE Up to 30 feet tall and wide

FLOWER COLOR Pink

SOIL Average, well-drained

LIGHT NEEDS Full sun to part shade

ATTRACTS Birds, hummingbirds, butterflies, bees

NATIVE PLANT TIP

Hybrid coneflowers come in orange, yellow, and even green, but the native pink varieties provide the best benefits to wildlife.

NATIVE PLANT TIP

Look for a serviceberry native to your area. A good choice in the Midwest is running serviceberry, *Amelanchier stolonifera*. Along the Pacific coast, try Saskatoon service-berry, *Amelanchier alnifolia*.

Enjoy the berries raw or in jam. They taste a bit like blueberries.

Serviceberry
Amelanchier arborea

You can grow serviceberry as a tree or shrub, depending on the variety you choose and how you prune it. It's a favorite with gardeners because of the steady supply of berries, which draw birds and other wildlife. Plus, it provides good shelter throughout the year.

PLANT TYPE Perennial

HARDINESS Zones 3 to 9

SIZE Up to 25 feet tall and wide

FLOWER COLOR White

SOIL Medium, well-drained

LIGHT NEEDS Full sun to part shade

ATTRACTS Birds, hummingbirds, butterflies, bees

Shasta daisy
Leucanthemum ×superbum

This classic daisy works in so many different settings, including perennial beds, edges and borders, hummingbird gardens, and even in containers. From its long-blooming and nectar-rich flowers to seeds that dry out for the birds later in the season, it offers plenty of benefits to wildlife.

PLANT TYPE Perennial
HARDINESS Zones 5 to 9
SIZE Up to 4 feet tall and 3 feet wide
FLOWER COLOR White
SOIL Dry to medium, well-drained
LIGHT NEEDS Full sun
ATTRACTS Birds, hummingbirds, butterflies, bees

Divide Shasta daisies in early spring so they'll keep multiplying, which they'll do prolifically. In a few years, you could have a mass of bright white daisies.

In fall, cut off some sunflower heads and tuck them away in a dry shed, garage, or basement. Then put them outside in winter, near your other feeders, to provide natural feed when many birds often need it most.

Sunflower
Helianthus annuus

Sunflowers produce the classic flowers that bear abundant edible seeds that birds (and, perhaps, you) love. They're one of the easiest plants to grow from seed and can give birds quite the buffet from summer and into fall. There are so many sunflower varieties to choose from, including the mammoth types with large seeds. The shorter and smaller sunflowers also offer nutritious meals for birds. For the best results, mix several types of sunflowers in one garden bed. Plant them densely in rows to create a colorful seasonal privacy screen.

PLANT TYPE Annual
HARDINESS Annual throughout most areas
SIZE Up to 10 feet tall and 3 feet wide
FLOWER COLOR Yellow, red, bicolor
SOIL Average, well-drained
LIGHT NEEDS Full sun
ATTRACTS Birds, hummingbirds, butterflies, bees

If you have an area where it's hard to get plants to grow, try an ornamental grass like switchgrass. It's often easier to get established than perennial flowers and will come back year after year.

Switchgrass
Panicum virgatum

Here's an example of a grass that can have as much color and interest as a flowering perennial. Its foliage is bright green in spring, red to deep purple through summer and early fall, and finally, tawny in winter. Just as most of your garden flowers are peaking in color, it will start to turn. This makes it a perfect choice for containers or perennial beds because you can keep your garden going. Its seeds appeal to birds, and if you leave it up in winter, it'll continue to offer them both food and protection from the winter elements.

PLANT TYPE Perennial

HARDINESS Zones 5 to 9

SIZE Up to 6 feet tall and 3 feet wide

FLOWER COLOR Not significant but small and pink

SOIL Average, medium to wet

LIGHT NEEDS Full sun to part shade

ATTRACTS Birds

Viburnum
Viburnum

Here's another berry-producing shrub that has appeal throughout the year. In spring, its beautiful and fragrant flowers attract hummingbirds, butterflies, and bees, and its berries will feed birds and other wildlife throughout the winter. These attributes make the viburnums really strong backyard food sources for wildlife.

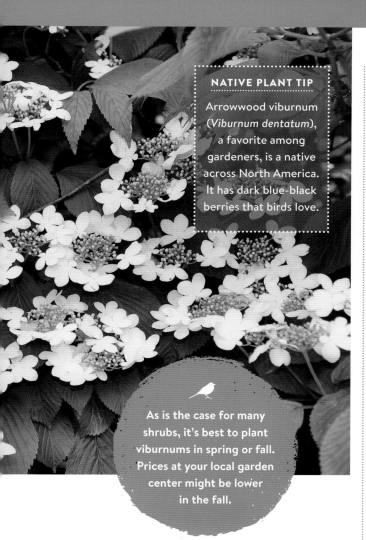

NATIVE PLANT TIP

Arrowwood viburnum (*Viburnum dentatum*), a favorite among gardeners, is a native across North America. It has dark blue-black berries that birds love.

As is the case for many shrubs, it's best to plant viburnums in spring or fall. Prices at your local garden center might be lower in the fall.

PLANT TYPE Perennial

HARDINESS Zones 3 to 9

SIZE Up to 15 feet tall and 12 feet wide

FLOWER COLOR White

SOIL Medium, well-drained

LIGHT NEEDS Full sun to part shade

ATTRACTS Birds, hummingbirds, butterflies, bees

Try pairing several female winterberry shrubs with a single male to get the most berries. Winterberry is also known as holly.

Winterberry
Ilex verticillata

Winterberry lives up to its name by providing a steady source of berries for birds during some of the coldest months of the year. It's dioecious, so you'll need to plant at least one male and one female shrub to get berries, which are borne on the female plants. If you're not sure how to buy a male plant, check online or at your local garden center. Once you get the right mix, you'll provide winterberries for birds for many years.

PLANT TYPE Perennial

HARDINESS Zones 3 to 9

SIZE Up to 12 feet tall and wide

FLOWER COLOR Not significant

SOIL Medium to wet, slightly acidic

LIGHT NEEDS Full sun to part shade

ATTRACTS Birds

Look for specific cultivars with red, pink, or yellow flowers to add color and variety to your yard.

Yew
Taxus ×media

The yew family offers many types of evergreen varieties. *Taxus ×media* is a cross between English and Japanese yews. It's very forgiving for most home gardeners; use it in hard-to-grow spots, and prune and shape it as you'd like. It produces fruit that birds love and will give you solid, year-round color.

PLANT TYPE Perennial
HARDINESS Zones 4 to 7
SIZE Up to 20 feet tall and 12 feet wide
FLOWER COLOR Insignificant
SOIL Medium, well-drained
LIGHT NEEDS Full sun to full shade
ATTRACTS Birds

Yews are fairly forgiving when it comes to pruning. Prune in late winter or early spring, just before new growth starts.

Yarrow
Achillea millefolium

Yarrow offers great nectar for hummingbirds, bees, and butterflies, and it is also a good source of seeds for birds. It's drought-tolerant and does well in average to poor soil. It does have a tendency to spread, and some gardeners even see it as aggressive. But if you can contain it or give it space in a wildflower garden, then it's a great, long-term investment that will attract wildlife to your yard.

PLANT TYPE Perennial
HARDINESS Zones 3 to 8
SIZE Up to 3 feet tall and wide
FLOWER COLOR White
SOIL Average to poor, well-drained, sandy, loamy
LIGHT NEEDS Full sun
ATTRACTS Birds, hummingbirds, butterflies, bees

To save zinnia seeds for next year, let the seed heads dry completely. Gently shake the seeds onto a dry cloth and then into a paper envelope. Write the variety on the envelope. Store in a cool, dry place.

Zinnia
Zinnia elegans

A single packet of zinnia seeds can give you dozens of blooms to bring in hummingbirds, butterflies, and bees. This popular annual is easy to grow from seed and packs a big punch, with vibrant blooms that can last through fall. Give zinnias sunshine and water, and they won't disappoint.

PLANT TYPE Annual

HARDINESS Annual throughout the United States

SIZE Up to 4 feet tall and 1 foot wide

FLOWER COLOR Orange, pink, purple, red, white, yellow, green, multicolor

SOIL Medium, well-drained

LIGHT NEEDS Full sun

ATTRACTS Hummingbirds, butterflies, bees

I Want to Attract
HUMMINGBIRDS

Hummingbirds are among the most coveted backyard visitors. If you've never had them, you want them. And if you've been lucky enough to attract them, you'll do everything you can to bring them back year after year.

Start by planting flowers that produce lots of nectar, the natural food for hummingbirds, as well as bees, butterflies, and other important beneficial insects. You might think that all flowers produce similar amounts and kinds of nectar, but that's not the case; some are definitely better than others. That's especially true of native plants.

In addition to planting flowers, there are plenty of other ways you can create a space that will welcome hummingbirds to your garden.

KEEP FEEDERS CLEAN AND FULL

To attract hummingbirds for the first time (or to bring them back), it definitely helps to provide sugar-water feeders. These often act like magnets for hummingbirds, because they ensure a consistent source of nectar. It's one thing to put a single feeder up and fill it, but it's another thing to keep it clean and filled throughout the season. This can take work, but it's incredibly important. Ants and other bugs can quickly make a mess out of a feeder, so it's worth investing in an ant moat if your feeder doesn't have one. Plus, keep your feeder filled so hummingbirds know they'll always find high-quality nectar in your yard. To prevent the spread of pathogens, it's essential to wash the feeder regularly in hot, soapy water and rinse and dry it thoroughly before refilling it.

OFFER MULTIPLE FEEDERS WHEN POSSIBLE

After you've mastered one feeder, put up another one—or more. Often, a single male hummingbird will try to dominate a feeder by chasing others away. This is especially true during the peak of the breeding season. If you put up additional feeders, preferably out of sight of the first one, you'll increase your chances of bringing in more hummingbirds. Be sure to keep all of these feeders clean and full.

PLAN A GARDEN THAT BLOOMS CONTINUOUSLY

It's so rewarding to be outside among your flowers and suddenly hear a hummingbird zoom by. If you're able to expand the blooming season in your backyard, you'll have an even greater chance of attracting hummingbirds. For instance, early bloomers such as bleeding hearts and columbine can be exactly what you need to capture the attention of these little birds as they migrate north. Flowers that bloom into late summer, like petunias or zinnias, will be important food sources for those that fly south for the winter.

USE THE COLOR RED TO YOUR ADVANTAGE

There's a reason so many hummingbird feeders have red on them. They are definitely drawn to this color, which is related to the dense concentration of cones in the birds' retinas. You can make this work for you. Start by choosing a feeder that's red or has some red elements on it. If yours doesn't already have red on it, consider adding something red, like a bow or another decorative element. Also, definitely incorporate some red flowers into your flower beds, containers, and hanging baskets.

OFFER EXTRAS TO INCREASE YOUR CHANCE OF SUCCESS

If you want to go all out to bring hummingbirds to your yard, here are a few extra things to try. First, hummingbirds like water and are especially drawn to mists. Look into a misting fountain or even a small solar fountain—the movement of water likely will attract them. Also, you can buy or make a hummingbird "swing." This looks a lot like a perch you'd find for a pet bird, and when you hang it from a tree, it gives them a place to rest.

STAY CONSISTENT DURING HUMMINGBIRD SEASON

One of the best things you can do is be consistent. When hummingbirds establish a territory, they often stay there for an extended period and return year after year. If you don't give them reliable sources of sugar water and nectar, they might leave to find other sources and never return. So, develop a routine, and stick to it. If you plan to go on vacation, have someone keep your plants watered and your sugar-water feeders filled.

TIMING CAN MAKE A BIG DIFFERENCE

It can be frustrating to repeatedly try—and fail—to attract hummingbirds. If this has been the case for you, your best bet is to work hard to implement these best practices during the spring and fall migrations. In spring, you might get some hummingbirds that want to establish territories for the first time. You especially want to appeal to them because they might decide to make your backyard their home every year. In late summer and early fall, you might notice juvenile hummingbirds. These likely will be

Even though the color red attracts hummingbirds, research has shown that they're more drawn to flowers with high nectar content.

Many people worry that keeping feeders up year-round will interfere with a hummingbird's migration. This isn't true. These birds are smart enough to know when it's time to head south. If you keep a feeder up, you just might help a straggler who really needs some sugar-water fuel.

heading south for the first time. They'll be hungry and will stop wherever they can get an easy meal. This is the perfect time to put out an extra feeder.

PLANT NATIVES

Many flowers are developed and grown for benefits other than attracting hummingbirds. These include disease resistance and cold hardiness. It makes sense to incorporate such plants into your garden, but it's not always a great way to attract wildlife like hummingbirds. If you're considering planting new varieties in your yard, ensure that they're good for hummingbirds. If you're unsure, stick to natives if you can. They'll likely grow well and bring in the hummers.

Whether you do one, some, or all of these things, you should increase your chances of attracting hummingbirds to your yard. Now it's time to learn more about these little beauties and the plants they like. Get ready to create a hummingbird haven right outside your back door.

Discover Common Hummingbird Species

Here are some of the most common hummingbird species that might zip through your yard. Males tend to look different from females or juveniles, so look closely to identify what you're seeing. **»**

Allen's Hummingbird
Selasphorus sasin

Like its cousin, the rufous hummingbird, the Allen's hummingbird has beautiful copper coloring but it inhabits a much smaller range, mostly along the California coast. The males can have elaborate mating dances, highlighted by dives and squeals to lure females.

LENGTH Up to 3.5 inches

WINGSPAN Up to 4.3 inches

FEMALE MARKINGS Bronze-green body, coppery sides, reddish spotting on throat

MALE MARKINGS Similar to female but brighter overall; copper tail, eye patches, and chest; distinctive reddish-orange throat

SOUNDS Ticking sounds when foraging, fighting for territory, or mating; humming sound in flight, similar to bumblebee

HABITAT Narrow band of coastal forest along Pacific Ocean

NESTING From 2 to 50 feet high in trees, shrubs

DIET Nectar, sugar water, insects

RANGE Southern California and Arizona through Mexico

Some Allen's hummingbirds will stay in Southern California year-round. Those that migrate are among the earliest hummingbirds to return from their winter grounds, sometimes as early as January.

The Anna's hummingbird was named after Anna Masséna, Duchess of Rivoli. She was the daughter of a military general and a prestigious woman in Europe. While most hummingbirds migrate, Anna's hummers will stay in their area year-round.

Anna's hummingbird
Calypte anna

If you live in the western United States and are fortunate enough to live in this popular bird's range, you might see it year-round. While it's slightly larger than the ruby-throated, it's still very small—about the size of a ping-pong ball.

LENGTH Up to 3.9 inches

WINGSPAN Up to 4.7 inches

FEMALE MARKINGS Bright green back, crown; white-and-gray underparts

MALE MARKINGS Similar to female but with bright red throat coloring that wraps around top of head

SOUNDS Males "chip" and females sometimes respond, especially during mating season; both sexes make humming sound when flying

HABITAT Backyards, parks, woods, savannas, coastal areas

NESTING Prefer oak, sycamore, eucalyptus trees but also nest in other trees, shrubs

DIET Nectar, sugar water, insects

RANGE Far western United States, including California, Oregon, Washington, and many parts of the Southwest

This black-throated hummingbird uses its tongue to drink nectar from flowers. It does this at a rate of about 15 licks per second!

Black-chinned hummingbird
Archilochus alexandri

At first glance, black-chinned hummingbirds might look a little dull, but if you catch them at the right angle or in just the right light, both males' and females' feathers appear shiny and iridescent. These hummers are well-adapted to backyards, so they might visit your flowers and feeders regularly.

LENGTH Up to 3.5 inches

WINGSPAN Up to 4.3 inches

FEMALE MARKINGS Green back, white or grayish-white underside, pale throat

MALE MARKINGS Similar to females, except black throat with purple base that may sparkle

SOUNDS Variety of chipping sounds, humming sound while flying

HABITAT Diverse, including deserts, mountains, parks, backyards

NESTING Made of plant down and spider silk, located 6 to 12 feet high in a tree

DIET Nectar, sugar water, insects

RANGE Large area of western United States; will nest as far north as Washington and Canada; year-round in parts of the far Southwest

Broad-tailed hummingbird

Selasphorus platycercus

This hummingbird looks a lot like the ruby-throated, but it has a completely different range in the West. If you see this hummingbird perched, you'll understand its name, because the tail often extends beyond the wing feathers when it's resting.

LENGTH Up to 3.5 inches

WINGSPAN Up to 5.25 inches

FEMALE MARKINGS Bright green above, white chest, green spots on throat

MALE MARKINGS Similar to females, but with magenta throat patches and white-tipped feathers that are visible in flight

SOUNDS Variety of chipping sounds when foraging or fighting for territory; loud humming sound when in flight, similar to the sound of a cricket chirping

HABITAT Wide range, including meadows, forests, shrub habitats

NESTING Up to 5 feet high in evergreens, aspens, willows, or thickets, sometimes using materials from other birds' nests

DIET Nectar, sugar water, insects

RANGE Large part of the West, particularly Arizona, Colorado, Nevada, New Mexico, Utah

Like all hummingbirds, the broad-tailed protects itself from cold temperatures by entering a state of torpor. To do this, it lowers its metabolism and body temperature. Sometimes you'll even see one hanging upside down, unmoving, but be mindful not to disturb it.

After mating, ruby-throated males leave fairly quickly. Females do most of the work to build the nest and tend the young.

Ruby-throated hummingbird

Archilochus colubris

This is the only hummingbird that travels to the eastern half of the United States. It's very well-known and popular among gardeners. Its breeding and nesting range is quite large, so it's common to see it throughout the summer.

LENGTH Up to 3.5 inches

WINGSPAN Up to 4.3 inches

FEMALE MARKINGS Bright green back, crown; white-and-gray underparts

MALE MARKINGS Similar to female but with bright red throat

SOUNDS Males "chip" and females sometimes respond, especially during mating season; both sexes make humming sounds when flying

HABITAT Open woodlands, edges of forests, backyards, meadows, grasslands

NESTING Thimble-sized; high in trees; made of thistle and dandelion down, woven together with spider's silk

DIET Nectar, sugar water, insects

RANGE Eastern United States from late spring to late summer

Rufous hummingbird

Selasphorus rufus

Rufous hummingbirds have a reputation for fiercely defending their territory. If they find a good source of nectar from flowers, they can go to great lengths to keep other birds out. Look for these hummingbirds especially during migrations.

LENGTH Up to 3.5 inches

WINGSPAN Up to 4.3 inches

FEMALE MARKINGS Green with rufous spots on tail, throat, sides

MALE MARKINGS Bright orange back, rufous-and-white underside, red/rusty throat

SOUNDS Both sexes: chipping sounds to warn of predators; humming sound while flying; tend to be louder than many other hummingbirds

HABITAT Yards, parks, forests, meadows, areas with shrubs

NESTING Nests about 2 inches wide; up to 30 feet high in trees

DIET Nectar, sugar water, insects

RANGE One of the widest ranges for hummingbirds in North America, primarily in the western United States but occasionally along the eastern shore of the Gulf of Mexico

Rufous hummingbirds make one of the longest migrations of any bird. Some travel from Mexico to Alaska to nest—nearly 4,000 miles one way!

OTHER NORTH AMERICAN HUMMINGBIRDS

If your garden offers hummers' favorite flowering plants, you might see some of these less-common birds in your backyard, especially if you live in the western United States. Occasionally, a stray western species will end up in the East.

Costa's hummingbird

Calliope hummingbird

Buff-bellied hummingbird

Broad-billed hummingbird

HUMMINGBIRD PLANT RECOMMENDATIONS

By planting the right flowers, you can help support and protect hummingbird populations across North America. In turn, this will help increase your chances of seeing these amazing birds on your porch, deck, or patio. Here are some of the best flowers you can grow to bring hummingbirds into your yard.

Pinch off and deadhead flowers as they fade. This will encourage asters to produce blooms as long as possible.

Aster
Symphyotrichum novae-angliae

These daisy-like flowers will fill your garden with life and color throughout summer and early fall. Each plant produces dozens of blooms with bold, yellow centers. They are one of the most reliable bloomers in the garden, coming back strong year after year. Plus, as the plants get older, you can split them (do this in spring) and share them with other gardeners.

PLANT TYPE Perennial

HARDINESS Zones 3 to 8

SIZE Up to 6 feet tall and 3 feet wide

FLOWER COLOR Pink, purple, white, blue

SOIL Moist, rich

LIGHT NEEDS Full sun to part shade

ATTRACTS Hummingbirds, butterflies, bees

Bleeding heart
Lamprocapnos spectabilis

This hard-working flower is reliable, coming back year after year even in cold regions. It blooms early, so it's great for hummingbirds looking for nectar when they first arrive during spring migration. It's also popular with gardeners because it thrives in shade.

PLANT TYPE Perennial
HARDINESS Zones 3 to 9
SIZE Up to 3 feet tall and wide
FLOWER COLOR Pink, white
SOIL Average, well-drained
LIGHT NEEDS Part to full shade
ATTRACTS Hummingbirds, butterflies, bees

Bellflowers are a common flower to give as a thank-you gift.

Bellflower
Campanula americana

While there are many bellflower varieties, this one is the best for attracting hummingbirds. It grows several feet tall and has plenty of beautiful blooms from mid- to late summer. It's one of the few flowers in a true blue shade, though some cultivars are deeper blue than others. If it doesn't do well as a perennial in your garden, try growing it as an annual and/or in containers.

PLANT TYPE Perennial, annual
HARDINESS Zones 4 to 7
SIZE Up to 6 feet tall and 2 feet wide
FLOWER COLOR Blue, purple
SOIL Moist, well-drained
LIGHT NEEDS Full sun to part shade
ATTRACTS Hummingbirds, butterflies, bees

As the name indicates, bleeding heart's blooms definitely are heart-shaped, but they also resemble a hairstyle from the 1960s. (Think Ginger from the TV show *Gilligan's Island!*)

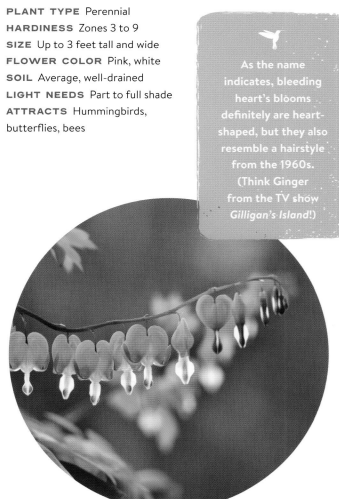

Calibrachoa
Calibrachoa spp.

These look like miniature petunias although they're not related to them. One of the most popular options for containers and hanging baskets, calibrachoas grow beautifully alone or mixed with other plants. They really are some of the most hardy and forgiving plants; in most zones they usually last for months, and in zones 9 to 11 they're perennials. Their long blooming season is great for attracting hummingbirds from spring through early fall. They're also called million bells and superbells.

PLANT TYPE Annual

HARDINESS Perennial in zones 9 to 11

SIZE Up to 1 foot tall and 2 feet wide

FLOWER COLOR Various colors, including bicolor, pink, purple, red, yellow, white

SOIL Moist, well-drained

LIGHT NEEDS Full sun

ATTRACTS Hummingbirds, butterflies, bees

These have a tendency to trail, which is why they're popular in hanging baskets. Unlike petunias, which benefit from deadheading, calibrachoas drop their flowers after blooming.

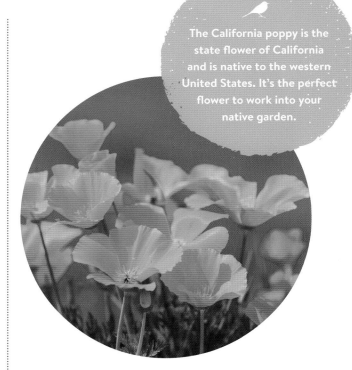

The California poppy is the state flower of California and is native to the western United States. It's the perfect flower to work into your native garden.

California poppy
Eschscholzia californica

Try California poppies in those harder-to-grow spaces or areas that don't get a lot of water, and you might be surprised by how well they do. You often see them growing along roads or in ditches in the western United States. More is better with this one, so grow an abundance from seed in early spring and you'll give hummingbirds lots of the nectar they crave.

PLANT TYPE Perennial, annual

HARDINESS Zones 6 to 10

SIZE Up to 2 feet tall and wide

FLOWER COLOR Orange to orange-yellow

SOIL Sandy, well-drained

LIGHT NEEDS Full sun

ATTRACTS Hummingbirds, butterflies, bees

Color-specific gardens are popular and stunning. Pair cardinal flowers with other red favorites like bee balm and zinnia to create a bright and bold display that will attract hummingbirds.

Cardinal flower
Lobelia cardinalis

Cardinal flower is native to much of the United States, and you'll often see it growing in the wild, especially along rivers, streams, and swamps. It likes a lot of moisture, so keep this in mind if you put it in your yard. With its combination of deep red flowers and tubular blooms, it's a must-have for any hummingbird garden.

PLANT TYPE Perennial

HARDINESS Zones 3 to 9

SIZE Up to 4 feet tall and 2 feet wide

FLOWER COLOR Red, white, pink

SOIL Rich, medium, wet

LIGHT NEEDS Full sun to part shade

ATTRACTS Hummingbirds, butterflies, bees

Pinch off any spent flowers to encourage new blooms.

Columbine
Aquilegia canadensis

Here's another native flower that is great for hummingbird gardens. Also an early bloomer, columbine often offers a good nectar source when other plants are just getting going. Once you have this plant established, it's reliable and will come back year after year.

PLANT TYPE Perennial

HARDINESS Zones 3 to 8

SIZE Up to 3 feet tall and 2 feet wide

FLOWER COLOR Light-pink-and-yellow, red-and-yellow

SOIL Medium, well-drained

LIGHT NEEDS Full sun to part shade

ATTRACTS Hummingbirds, butterflies, bees

NATIVE PLANT TIP

Columbines are native across North America. Depending on where you live, they might be called eastern red, western red, crimson, or Canadian columbine.

Coral bells
Heuchera spp.

If you haven't discovered coral bells, now is the time. They are shade-tolerant plants whose tiny blooms shoot out on long stems. You wouldn't think they'd be large enough to attract hummingbirds, but they are. Many gardeners grow coral bells for their gorgeous foliage, which ranges from orange to black, green, purple, red, silver, and yellow.

NATIVE PLANT TIP

Look for the botanical name, *Heuchera americana*, which is the coral bell native to North America.

There are many cultivars of coral bells, so research the diverse combinations of foliage and flower color to find your favorites.

PLANT TYPE Perennial

HARDINESS Zones 4 to 9

SIZE Up to 3 feet tall and 2 feet wide

FLOWER COLOR Many colors, including red, pink, white

SOIL Rich, well-drained

LIGHT NEEDS Full sun to full shade

ATTRACTS Hummingbirds, butterflies, bees

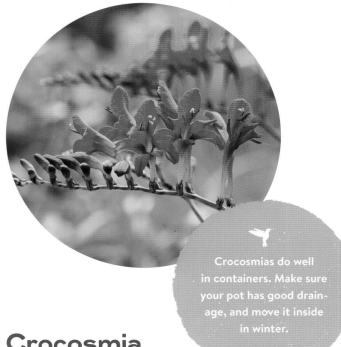

Crocosmias do well in containers. Make sure your pot has good drainage, and move it inside in winter.

Crocosmia
Crocosmia spp.

These long-blooming flowers, which grow from bulbs, welcome hummingbirds back to your area in early summer and provide a good source of nectar for nesting females. Although their flowers somewhat resemble gladioli, crocosmias actually are in the iris family. Another common name is montbretia. Crocosmias reliably add bold splashes of red to your garden, year after year. They work great in groups, especially for borders.

PLANT TYPE Perennial bulb

HARDINESS Zones 5 to 9

SIZE Up to 3 feet tall and wide

FLOWER COLOR Red, yellow, orange

SOIL Average, well-drained

LIGHT NEEDS Full sun to part shade

ATTRACTS Hummingbirds, butterflies, bees

Do you like double blooms? Do you prefer flowers with great fragrance? Indulge your fantasies with dahlias. They come in dozens of different sizes, colors, and shapes.

Delphinium
Delphinium spp.

If you live in a colder area and don't have extremely hot summers, put delphiniums on your list. Also known as a butterfly favorite, they are perfect for bringing in hummingbirds throughout the summer. They're a little more finicky than some perennials, but once you get the hang of them, they'll be stunning additions to your yard.

PLANT TYPE Perennial
HARDINESS Zones 3 to 7
SIZE Up to 6 feet tall and 3 feet wide
FLOWER COLOR Blue, pink, purple, white
SOIL Average, well-drained
LIGHT NEEDS Full sun to part shade
ATTRACTS Hummingbirds, butterflies, bees

Dahlia
Dahlia spp.

Dahlias are some of the most showy flowers you can grow. They're available in many different types, with quirky names like 'Dinner Plate' and 'Lollipop', and some flowers can be more than a foot across! They're grown from tubers and they tend to like warmer climates, but if you live in a colder region, don't worry: just dig them up in fall and replant them in spring.

PLANT TYPE Perennial
HARDINESS Zones 7 to 10 (and lower with modifications)
SIZE Up to 6 feet tall and 3 feet wide
FLOWER COLOR Many colors, including orange, pink, purple, red, white, yellow
SOIL Medium, well-drained
LIGHT NEEDS Full sun
ATTRACTS Hummingbirds, butterflies, bees

Delphiniums come in a wide range of heights, from dwarf varieties that grow only a couple of feet tall to larger ones that reach up to six feet. They are poisonous to both humans and animals, so be aware if you plant them in your yard.

Flowering tobacco
Nicotiana alata

The star-shaped, tubular blooms of flowering tobacco are like magnets to hummingbirds. Its fragrant flowers are quite attractive to other wildlife, too. Sometimes it will benefit from staking, especially when you're trying to get it established.

PLANT TYPE Annual for most

HARDINESS Perennial in zones 10 and 11

SIZE Up to 5 feet tall and 2 feet wide

FLOWER COLOR Green, pink, red, white, yellow

SOIL Rich, moist, well-drained

LIGHT NEEDS Full sun to part shade

ATTRACTS Hummingbirds, butterflies, bees

Flowering tobacco is in the same plant family as the tobacco plant used in cigarettes and cigars. As its botanical name indicates, *Nicotiana* contains a concentration of nicotine.

If you're feeling thrifty, dig up the tuberous roots in fall and save them to plant next year. Also, all parts of this plant are poisonous, so keep it away from kids and pets.

Foxglove
Digitalis purpurea

Foxgloves have beautiful tiered blooms that get bigger from top to bottom. The tubular flowers are a favorite with hummingbirds, so you might see a hummer with its bill deep in your foxgloves. The plants reseed easily, and you'll soon find one or two plants turning into five, ten, or more.

PLANT TYPE Perennial

HARDINESS Zones 4 to 8

SIZE Up to 5 feet tall and 3 feet wide

FLOWER COLOR Pink, purple, white

SOIL Average, well-drained

LIGHT NEEDS Full sun to part shade

ATTRACTS Hummingbirds, butterflies, bees

Foxgloves are great plants to use in borders or the backs of flower beds because they do such a nice job of framing the garden.

Four o'clock
Mirabilis jalapa

Native to Peru, this plant produces exotic-looking flowers that hummingbirds love. This is a popular plant to use alone or mixed with other hummingbird favorites in containers or in hanging baskets. Its long bloom time makes it a great choice throughout the summer.

PLANT TYPE Annual for most

HARDINESS Perennial in zones 9 to 11

SIZE Up to 3 feet tall and wide

FLOWER COLOR Magenta, pink, red, white, yellow

SOIL Wide range of well-drained soils

LIGHT NEEDS Full sun to part shade

ATTRACTS Hummingbirds, butterflies, bees

Geranium

Pelargonium spp.

Geraniums won't let you down. If there's an
area in your yard or patio where most plants
won't grow, try geraniums; they'll probably
thrive. If you water and deadhead them,
they'll probably look good from spring through
fall. The fact that they attract hummingbirds
is a bonus.

PLANT TYPE Annual for most

HARDINESS Perennial in zones 10 and 11

SIZE Up to 3 feet tall and wide

FLOWER COLOR Bicolor, orange, pink, purple,
red, white

SOIL Wide range, well-drained

LIGHT NEEDS Full sun to part shade

ATTRACTS Hummingbirds, butterflies, bees

Deadhead your geraniums
by pinching off faded blooms
and you'll get many
more flowers.

It can be overwhelming to decide between the hundreds of hosta options available. Read the descriptions carefully to ensure that the ones you like will also appeal to hummingbirds.

These plants do especially well in moist areas, so keep this in mind when you're planning your garden.

Hosta

Hosta spp.

You might think that hostas don't attract hummingbirds, but they do. They're well-known for their terrific foliage and ability to grow well in shade. Their small flowers also are full of nectar, so even if you have heavily shaded areas, try some hostas.

PLANT TYPE Perennial

HARDINESS Zones 3 to 8

SIZE Up to 4 feet tall and 6 feet wide

FLOWER COLOR Purple, white

SOIL Average, well-drained

LIGHT NEEDS Sun to shade

ATTRACTS Hummingbirds, butterflies, bees

Liatris

Liatris spicata

The upright, spiky blooms of liatris make a real statement in the garden. If you get close to them, you'll see that they're kind of fuzzy, which makes them popular with butterflies, bees, and hummingbirds. Enjoy their spectacular flowers while you can, because they don't bloom for long!

NATIVE PLANT TIP

Two other native *liatris* species to look for are cattail (*Liatris pycnostachya*) and dense liatris (*Liatris spicata*).

The plant was named *Pulmonaria* because it was used as a remedy for lung diseases in the sixteenth and seventeenth centuries.

Lungwort
Pulmonaria spp.

This is another favorite with gardeners who have a lot of shade because it's easy to grow and reliable, even in areas that get almost no direct sunlight. Lungwort often has interesting spotted or variegated foliage that can stay green into fall and winter. Even though the flowers are small, they do attract hummingbirds.

PLANT TYPE Perennial

HARDINESS Zones 3 to 8

SIZE Up to 1 foot tall and 2 feet wide

FLOWER COLOR Blue, pink, purple, white

SOIL Moist, well-drained

LIGHT NEEDS Part sun to full shade

ATTRACTS Hummingbirds, butterflies, bees

PLANT TYPE Perennial

HARDINESS Zones 3 to 8

SIZE Up to 4 feet tall and 2 feet wide

FLOWER COLOR Purple

SOIL Average, well-drained

LIGHT NEEDS Full sun

ATTRACTS Hummingbirds, butterflies, bees

Lupines sometimes struggle in the heat, so if you live in a colder region, this is a great option for you.

Penstemon

Penstemon spp.

Penstemons' tubular red flowers are among hummingbirds' favorites. Penstemons are hardy perennials whose blooms keep going all summer. They work beautifully in a perennial garden designed to attract hummingbirds.

PLANT TYPE Perennial

HARDINESS Zones 3 to 10

SIZE Up to 2 feet tall and 4 feet wide

FLOWER COLOR Red, pink, purple, blue, white

SOIL Well-drained, sandy

LIGHT NEEDS Part shade to full sun

ATTRACTS Hummingbirds, butterflies, bees

Lupine

Lupinus spp.

Hummingbirds will stop by your blooming lupines in late spring. These tall, regal flowers offer beautiful colors and enticing fragrances, and after the flowers fade, good foliage for the rest of the growing season. The flower clusters make a big impact, especially if you put several plants close together. Lupines grow throughout North America, even as far north as the Arctic.

PLANT TYPE Perennial

HARDINESS Zones 4 to 8

SIZE Up to 4 feet tall and 2 feet wide

FLOWER COLOR Purple, blue, pink, white, red, yellow, bicolor

SOIL Fertile, moist, well-drained

LIGHT NEEDS Part shade to full sun

ATTRACTS Hummingbirds, butterflies, bees

NATIVE PLANT TIP

One of the best-known native lupines is the blue lupine (*Lupinus perennis*).

There are many native penstemons. Ask people at your local garden center or native plant society to recommend cultivars that will best meet your needs.

NATIVE PLANT TIP

Other native penstemon species to look for include coral penstemon (*Penstemon superbus*), desert penstemon (*Penstemon pseudo-spectabilis*), and fire-cracker penstemon (*Penstemon eatonii*).

You can propagate pentas easily by taking cuttings in spring and rooting them to create new plants.

Penta
Pentas lanceolata

Pentas, or Egyptian stars, are native to warm, tropical habitats, and are popular annuals that can add bold colors to your backyard or patio. Pentas will perform all summer if you water and deadhead them regularly. Perfect when planted alone in containers and paired with other nectar-rich annuals, pentas' bright, star-shaped flowers will bring plenty of wildlife to your yard.

PLANT TYPE Annual

HARDINESS Annual for most or can overwinter year-round in warm climates

SIZE Up to 6 feet tall and 3 feet wide

FLOWER COLOR Pink, red, white, lavender, purple

SOIL Medium, well-drained

LIGHT NEEDS Part sun to full sun

ATTRACTS Hummingbirds, butterflies, bees

Combine petunias with their look-alikes, calibrachoas, for a massive amount of flowers all summer and into fall.

Red hot poker
Kniphofia uvaria

The red hot poker is the kind of flower you see and immediately know you have to grow it. It has such a striking look, with its layers of tubular flowers that often change color from top to bottom. Although the bloom time sometimes can be short for this beauty, when it's in full flower mode the hummingbirds will love it.

PLANT TYPE Perennial

HARDINESS Zones 5 to 9

SIZE Up to 5 feet tall and 2 feet wide

FLOWER COLOR Red, yellow, orange

SOIL Medium, well-drained

LIGHT NEEDS Full sun to part shade

ATTRACTS Hummingbirds, butterflies, bees

Petunia
Petunia spp.

Petunias are one of the most popular annuals to use in containers and hanging baskets. With good reason, too, because they're easy to grow throughout the United States; are long-blooming; and attract hummingbirds, bees, and butterflies. They're also very forgiving if you don't have the perfect soil or water conditions. Plus, with all the colors available, you can create just the look you want.

PLANT TYPE Annual

HARDINESS Annual throughout North America

SIZE Up to 2 feet tall and 3 feet wide

FLOWER COLOR Most colors, including bicolor

SOIL Medium, well-drained

LIGHT NEEDS Part shade to full sun

ATTRACTS Hummingbirds, butterflies, bees

To keep this perennial performing at its best, cut the flower stems back in fall and divide them every few years.

You can grow Rose of Sharon like a vine or prune it to be more like a shrub.

Rose of Sharon

Hibiscus syriacus

Rose of Sharon's name is deceptive. It's not in the rose family, but the blooms of some cultivars can be just as beautiful and fragrant as traditional roses. Actually, this perennial with the tropical-looking flowers is closely related to the popular garden hibiscus. It's easy to establish for most gardeners in zones 5 to 8. Flowers bloom for a long time, which makes them perfect for attracting hummingbirds.

PLANT TYPE Perennial

HARDINESS Zones 5 to 8

SIZE Up to 12 feet tall and 10 feet wide

FLOWER COLOR Pink, purple, blue, white, bicolor

SOIL Medium, well-drained

LIGHT NEEDS Part shade to full sun

ATTRACTS Hummingbirds, butterflies, bees

NATIVE PLANT TIP

A good native salvia to grow in the Southeast is scarlet sage (*Salvia coccinea*).

Salvia is a popular container plant, especially when paired with other red favorites like petunias or pentas.

Salvia
Salvia spp.

Salvias comprise a huge group of plants in the sage family. There are many popular cultivars, from pineapple sage (*Salvia elegans*) to the popular red-blooming salvia or native autumn sage (*Salvia greggii*). Nearly all salvias are naturally great nectar sources. Keep them in sunny spots and water regularly to have blooms through early fall.

PLANT TYPE Annual

HARDINESS Annual for most, perennial in zones 8 to 10 and warmer climates

SIZE Up to 3 feet tall and wide

FLOWER COLOR Blue, purple, red

SOIL Medium, well-drained

LIGHT NEEDS Part shade to full sun

ATTRACTS Hummingbirds, butterflies, bees

Scarlet runner bean
Phaseolus coccineus

When you plant scarlet runner beans, you'll grow delicious veggies for your plate while also serving nectar to hummingbirds. These popular annuals have tender, edible beans similar to green beans. The vines, which feature red flowers, can climb to great heights on a fence or trellis. They're easy to grow from seeds and are perfect for your flower or veggie garden.

PLANT TYPE Perennial, annual

HARDINESS Perennial in zones 7 to 11, annual elsewhere

SIZE Up to 12 feet tall and 5 feet wide

FLOWER COLOR Red

SOIL Rich, organic, well-drained

LIGHT NEEDS Full sun

ATTRACTS Hummingbirds, butterflies, bees

Snapdragon
Antirrhinum majus

If you plant snapdragons, you'll get a lot of bang for your buck. They bloom for a long time in spring, take a break in summer, and then often bloom again in late summer and early fall. All you need to do is keep deadheading the flowers to encourage growth. And hummingbirds love their nectar!

Snapdragons often reseed themselves in warmer climates. You also can collect seeds late in the season to plant next year. Fortunately, they also perennialize in many parts of the United States.

PLANT TYPE Annual

HARDINESS Annual for most; perennial for some in zones 7 and up

SIZE Up to 3 feet tall and 1 foot wide

FLOWER COLOR White, yellow, orange, purple, pink, red, purple, bicolor

SOIL Moist, well-drained

LIGHT NEEDS Part shade to full sun

ATTRACTS Hummingbirds, butterflies, bees

You'll see flowers four to five weeks after planting. Pick the ripe beans to encourage new growth and flowering.

Wisteria
Wisteria frutescens

Here's another vine that will bring a lot of life to your garden if you can give it the space and support it needs. In addition to its gorgeous, long-lasting purple blooms, wisteria has an amazing fragrance. Wisteria is dazzling on pergolas and trellises. Once it's established, be sure to cut the fast-growing vine back each year to keep it manageable.

PLANT TYPE Perennial

HARDINESS Zones 5 to 9

SIZE Up to 8 feet tall and 30 feet wide

FLOWER COLOR Lilac, purple

SOIL Slightly acidic, well-drained

LIGHT NEEDS Part shade to full sun

ATTRACTS Hummingbirds, butterflies, bees

It can take a few years to get trumpet vine established and blooming, so don't give up if you don't have success right away.

Trumpet vine
Campsis radicans

Make sure you have the space and support for this perennial vine before you plant it because it can get quite big and heavy. If your site will work, then plant it and let it grow! It's a surefire draw for hummingbirds. Once established, it'll produce dozens of large blooms until late summer.

PLANT TYPE Perennial

HARDINESS Zones 4 to 9

SIZE Up to 40 feet tall and 20 feet wide

FLOWER COLOR Orange, scarlet, yellow

SOIL Medium, well-drained

LIGHT NEEDS Part shade to full sun

ATTRACTS Hummingbirds, butterflies, bees

Before you buy a wisteria, look closely at the botanical name to verify that the cultivar isn't invasive in your locale.

Yuccas like it dry, so don't overwater.

Yucca

Yucca filamentosa

This is one of the best plants for drought-tolerant areas. In addition, it's a great plant for hummingbirds. The large, white, bell-shaped flowers appear on tall stalks that shoot up from the middle of the plant. The flowers provide hummingbirds nectar for most of the summer.

PLANT TYPE Perennial

HARDINESS Zones 5 to 10

SIZE Up to 8 feet tall and 3 feet wide

FLOWER COLOR White

SOIL Sandy, well-drained

LIGHT NEEDS Part shade to full sun

ATTRACTS Hummingbirds, butterflies, bees

I Want to Garden for
BEES

When you plan a garden for bees, you'll see benefits for years to come. Not only are you helping support declining bee populations, but in turn, these insects will do an incredible job of pollinating your plants and flowers. Through this important step in the gardening process, the bees help you establish robust flower gardens, healthy veggies, strong trees and shrubs, and more.

The honeybee is definitely one of the most popular bee species gardeners seek out, but it's certainly not the only one you're likely to see in your yard. Luckily, when you focus on providing a few key garden elements, all the bees that live nearby will benefit from your efforts. Here are some of the top action items you can do to bring bees to your backyard.

AVOID SYNTHETIC PESTICIDES

Many bee species can fly up to 20 miles per hour.

When you create a wildlife-friendly yard, the best thing you can do is provide an organic growing environment. We rarely realize the amount of pesticides we're exposed to every day, whether in parks, fields, or yards. These can be detrimental to us and all other living things, especially bees, so when you're planning, planting, and maintaining your garden, be sure not to add any synthetic herbicides, fungicides, or pesticides. The number and effectiveness of organic products for weed and pest control have increased substantially. If you need these products, use them according to their labels. Your efforts could make a big difference in establishing and nurturing a strong bee population in your yard and surrounding areas.

FOCUS ON POLLEN-RICH PLANTS

Not all flowers are good pollen producers, and there are a couple of main reasons why. First, there's a large market for low-pollen flowers, especially for people who have allergies. Plant breeders have gotten better at developing successful new flower varieties, so there are many more options than there used to be. Often, these are selected for special features, like double blooms or appealing colors—rather than the benefits they provide for bees.

This means you'll want to seek out plants that are strong pollen producers. Be sure to read plants' labels and their descriptions in seed catalogs, gardening books, and other resources. If they're good for bees, there's a good chance the descriptions will say so. You also can ask your local gardening experts or staff at your garden center to recommend plants that will bring in the bees. They'll likely have good suggestions for your area.

Flowering plants are actually not a big cause of allergic reactions. Instead, when you suspect that a flower's pollen is causing your symptoms, the culprits may be plants like ragweed, trees, and grasses. So, don't necessarily avoid planting a pollen-bearing flowering plant that you and the bees love because you're afraid it might trigger allergies.

PLANT SPRING BLOOMERS

You're not going to see a lot of bees when it's cold because they'll be hunkered down in their hives or underground. When bees emerge early in the year, they need food sources. By providing spring blooms, you'll help establish your yard as a pollen-friendly, nectar-rich area, and bees will keep coming back for more. Better yet, try to have something they like blooming throughout the year.

FILL YOUR YARD WITH NATIVES

Bees have been pollinating flowers for millennia and have adapted to their preferred plants and growing conditions. When you focus on growing natives, you'll naturally attract native bees. State and local native plant societies provide substantial information about how to find, select, and care for good native plants.

GROW BLUE AND PURPLE FLOWERS

Researchers have found that bees all over the world tend to be more attracted to blue and purple flowers. This doesn't mean they won't be drawn to other colors, but by planting blues and purples, you should increase your chances of establishing a bee-friendly space. In addition to blue hues, scientists have discovered that bees are also attracted to the yellow spectrum. Purple and yellow are complementary colors, so why not fill your containers or garden areas with them?

Some bees appear in spring for only a few weeks before they tunnel down into the ground to nest, so it's especially important to provide flowers that bloom in early spring.

Bees are attracted to blue and purple because of their ability to see ultraviolet light.

Bees will sometimes eat their own honey. When it gets too thick, they'll thin it with water to make it drinkable again.

ADD WATER SOURCES

Bees need water, too. By adding a water source to your space, you're much more likely to attract bees. You can do this with a birdbath, shallow water dish, or even a hummingbird feeder filled with plain water. If you do offer bee- and bird-friendly water sources, be sure to clean and fill them with fresh water regularly. This will keep bees coming back for more.

LET YOUR GARDEN GO WILD

When attracting wildlife to your yard, you can achieve a lot by moving away from the perfectly manicured lawn and garden. Think about a wildflower field that's alive with birds, bees, and other animals that visit the many flowers growing in a small space. Try to replicate this in your garden. This freestyle approach will naturally bring in the bees because it's what they're used to in the wild.

Discover Common Backyard Bees

Here are some of the most common bees you might see buzzing around your backyard and stopping at flowers for nectar. As you expand your garden and add even more bee-friendly blooms, you can be sure you'll attract even more bee species. »

Alkali bees have an unusual ability to open an alfalfa flower by applying pressure to the bloom to snap open the keel of the flower.

Blueberry bees
Habropoda laboriosa

While this bee visits a large range of flowers, it's especially drawn to blueberries. It's active for a very short period, usually in early spring. During peak season, a single female bee might visit more than 600 flowers a day. She's responsible for the development of thousands of ripe blueberries!

SIZE ½ inch and longer
MARKINGS Similar to fuzzy bumblebee; male has yellow face
HABITAT Backyards, gardens
NESTING Long, vertical nests, usually in sandy soil
DIET Pollen, nectar
RANGE Primarily eastern United States

Alkali bees
Nomia melanderi

Alkali bees resemble honeybees. They're generally solitary, but females often build their complex underground nests in salty soil near others' nests. Look for the hundreds of tiny holes the females excavate in the ground.

SIZE ⁷⁄₁₆ inch
MARKINGS Similar to honeybees
HABITAT Deserts, semi-arid areas
NESTING Underground in alkaline soil, often near alfalfa fields
DIET Pollen, nectar
RANGE Western United States

While these bees look a lot like bumblebees, the male bees have yellow faces.

Bumblebees leave their scent on flowers they visit; this guides other bees to good food sources.

Carpenter bees
Ceratina

At first glance, this insect might look more like an ant than a bee. Also known as the small carpenter bee, you can find this flier across North America. It's easy to confuse with the large carpenter bee (scientific name *Xylocopa*), which is bigger but has a smaller range. In part, this bee gets its name because it often burrows into trees, decks, and other wood.

SIZE Under ½ inch

MARKINGS Dark metallic body, often with green sheen; male has white patches between its eyes

HABITAT Backyards, forests, other areas with wood

NESTING Tunnels in hollowed-out stems or twigs

DIET Pollen, nectar

RANGE Across North America

Bumblebees
Bombus

You can find more than 40 species of bumblebees in North America, though many populations have been on the decline recently. Bumblebees are unique because they often survive under conditions other bees can't tolerate, such as cold temperatures and high altitudes. Bumblebees are important pollinators for flowers, and they often favor blue or purple blooms.

SIZE Up to 1 inch

MARKINGS Black, hairy body with yellow patches

HABITAT Wide range, including backyards, meadows

NESTING Often underground in old animal burrows, usually in groups of 50 to 500

DIET Nectar, pollen

RANGE Throughout North America

The opening of a carpenter bee's home might be only one or two inches across, but its tunnel can be ten feet long or more.

There are more than 400 species of digger bees in the world, including more than 70 species in the United States. Many of these are concentrated in the West.

Digger bees
Anthophorini

If you see insects swarming just above the ground in early spring, there's a good chance they're a species of digger bees. They can do a lot of good for your garden and yard because they pollinate plants and prey upon harmful insects. They rarely sting or attack humans unless disturbed, so if you can find a way to live at peace with them, they can be great for your plants.

SIZE ¼ inch to ½ inch

MARKINGS Often dark with shiny metallic markings or yellow or white spots

HABITAT Backyards, gardens, forests

NESTING Tunnel of nests about 6 inches underground

DIET Pollen, nectar

RANGE All over the United States

A single honeybee colony might have more than 50,000 worker bees. The bees collectively visit about two million flowers to make a pound of honey.

Honeybees
Apis mellifera

The honeybee is one of the few bee species in the world that makes honey. It's also one of the most common backyard bees, buzzing around plants, collecting nectar, and pollinating blooms. When you see a honeybee in your backyard, there's a good chance it's part of a hive from a local colony. A single honeybee might visit more than 1,000 flowers in one day, so you'll always see them on the move.

SIZE About ½ inch
MARKINGS Brown body with yellow bands
HABITAT Gardens, woodlands, orchards, meadows
NESTING Hives made from wax secreted by abdominal glands
DIET Nectar, pollen
RANGE Throughout North America

Leafcutter bees
Megachile

This is a big family of bees! There are more than 200 subspecies of leafcutter bees throughout North America, and there's a good chance you can see one in your area. These little bees are known for their habit of cutting smooth, semicircular sections out of plant leaves to use for their nests. Like other bees, they also play the important role of pollinating flowers and other plants.

SIZE Under ½ inch
MARKINGS Small, dark body; striping on lower half
HABITAT Wide range, including backyards, wooded areas
NESTING In the soil of homes made by other insects
DIET Pollen, nectar
RANGE Across North America

Unlike a lot of bees that live in colonies, leafcutters are fairly solitary. They overwinter underground and then eat their way out of their nests in spring.

Mason bees are excellent pollinators—even more effective than honeybees. While many bees carry pollen on their legs, mason bees carry it on their abdomens.

Mason bees

Osmia

Many bee species won't use man-made nests or structures, but these mason bees sometimes do. You can create your own mason bee nesting box by drilling holes into a log, stump, or board. You'll easily find directions online. Mason bees emerge from their holes in fairly early spring; in just a few weeks, they gather the food they need to breed and overwinter and then reenter and seal their nesting holes with mud to protect themselves during winter. This bit of engineering is why they're called mason bees. To help them, ensure there's a good supply of mud near the nest.

SIZE ⅜ to ⅝ inch

MARKINGS Dark body, similar to a housefly, with blue-and-green flashes

HABITAT Backyards, wooded areas

NESTING Tunnels, including "bee hotels"

DIET Pollen, nectar

RANGE Across North America

Squash bees carry pollen on the hairs of their hind legs.

Sweat bees
Halictidae

Sweat bees make up the second largest family of bees, with more than 4,500 species spread across every continent, including throughout the United States. As their name suggests, sweat bees are attracted to sweat, so one might land on your arm on a hot summer day. They aren't aggressive, so a breeze or gentle movement usually will send them on their way.

SIZE ½ inch or less

MARKINGS Dark, often with metallic markings

HABITAT Gardens, forests, grasslands

NESTING Underground, often in clay soil and river banks

DIET Pollen, nectar

RANGE Throughout the United States

Squash bees
Peponapis and *Xenoglossa*

Other bees usually only buzz around squash plants, but it's the squash bee that actually gets in there and does the work of pollinating the flowers. They're critical in ensuring good harvests of squash and other veggies. These useful garden bees look a lot like honeybees. Though they're named for their attraction to squash plants, they regularly stop at other plants in the cucurbit family, including watermelons, pumpkins, and zucchini.

SIZE ½ inch and longer

MARKINGS Similar to, but larger than, a honeybee

HABITAT Backyards, gardens, wooded areas

NESTING Solitary females build single nests underground

DIET Pollen, nectar

RANGE Throughout North America

This bee is small, and people often confuse it with a housefly.

BEE PLANT RECOMMENDATIONS

Bees need our support. By planting a bee-friendly garden, you can help them benefit the environment. It's relatively easy to plan the nectar-rich garden bees rely on. Here are some flowers you may want to incorporate into your garden.

Abelia blooms on new wood, so trim the shrub heavily in winter or early spring before buds begin to emerge. This will ensure a steady supply of flowers.

Abelia
Abelia ×grandiflora

This shrub in the honeysuckle family has showy, fragrant flowers that start blooming in spring. Some cultivars bloom through summer and early fall. Leaves often turn purplish-brown in fall, which adds multi-season interest.

PLANT TYPE Perennial

HARDINESS Zones 5 to 9

SIZE Up to 6 feet tall and wide

FLOWER COLOR White, pink

SOIL Average, well-drained

LIGHT NEEDS Full sun to part shade

ATTRACTS Bees, butterflies, hummingbirds

If you look really closely, you'll see that this plant's ball-shaped bloom consists of many tiny star-shaped flowers.

Allium
Allium giganteum

This flower, a member of the onion family, adds a bright and beautiful spot of color in spring. Plant these bulbs much like you do tulips or daffodils—in the fall. There are many different allium options, and this giant variety is one of the most popular. The large, softball-sized flowers can be six inches wide or more.

PLANT TYPE Perennial
HARDINESS Zones 5 to 8
SIZE Up to 5 feet tall and 2 feet wide
FLOWER COLOR Purple
SOIL Average, well-drained
LIGHT NEEDS Full sun
ATTRACTS Bees, butterflies, birds, hummingbirds

Bee balm
Monarda

There's a good reason this flower has "bee" in its common name. It's one of the single best perennials to plant if you want to bring more bees to your garden. Plus, there are popular native options wherever you live in North America.

PLANT TYPE Perennial
HARDINESS Zones 4 to 9
SIZE Up to 5 feet tall and 3 feet wide
FLOWER COLOR Red, pink, purple, lavender
SOIL Medium, well-drained
LIGHT NEEDS Full sun to part shade
ATTRACTS Bees, birds, butterflies, hummingbirds

To keep your bee balm plants healthy and strong, divide them every few years. This will reduce overcrowding and improve air circulation, which can help prevent powdery mildew.

NATIVE PLANT TIP

This flower is native throughout North America. You might also see it called wild bergamot or monarda.

NATIVE PLANT TIP

This flower is part of the aster family, and it's native to most of North America.

Try deadheading blanket flowers when you start to see them fade. This can sometimes encourage another round of flowering.

Blanket flower

Gaillardia ×grandiflora

Even though blanket flowers are shorter perennials, they still have great power to bring in the bees and other wildlife. Blanket flowers are reliable, resilient blooms. Once you get them established, they'll likely come back year after year. You can try starting this one from seed. If you can pick a variety that's native to your area, that's even better.

PLANT TYPE Perennial

HARDINESS Zones 3 to 10

SIZE Up to 2 feet tall and 2 feet wide

FLOWER COLOR Mixture of yellow, orange, red

SOIL Medium, well-drained

LIGHT NEEDS Full sun

ATTRACTS Bees, birds, hummingbirds, butterflies

Buttonbush
Cephalanthus occidentalis

This low-maintenance shrub invites bees into your garden. Its unique spiky, ball-shaped blooms peak in late summer. It shouldn't require much pruning. If you don't plant it in dry soil, it'll be a reliable food source for bees for many years.

- - - - - - - -

PLANT TYPE Perennial

HARDINESS Zones 5 to 9

SIZE Up to 12 feet tall and 8 feet wide

FLOWER COLOR White

SOIL Moist, humus-rich soil

LIGHT NEEDS Full sun to part shade

ATTRACTS Bees, butterflies, hummingbirds

You'll often see buttonbush growing in the wild in wet, marshy areas. In fact, it can even survive flooding because it likes moisture so much.

Calendula
Calendula officinalis

This daisy-like plant looks a lot like the marigolds sold in garden centers, but it's actually a different flower. It's hardy and easy to grow, especially in containers and borders. If you pinch back the flowers, you can get blooms all summer long. It will also reseed on its own in warmer climates.

PLANT TYPE Annual for most areas

HARDINESS Zones 2 to 11

SIZE Up to 2 feet tall and wide

FLOWER COLOR Yellow, orange

SOIL Average, well-drained

LIGHT NEEDS Full sun to part shade

ATTRACTS Bees, butterflies, hummingbirds, birds

In areas with cold winters, you may want to protect candytuft with mulch or straw in the fall.

Candytuft
Iberis sempervirens

This low-growing perennial really draws bees and butterflies. Gardeners love planting it in borders and in front of taller plants like zinnias or coneflowers. As the flowers start to fade in spring or summer, trim it back to encourage it to bloom again in fall.

PLANT TYPE Perennial

HARDINESS Zones 3 to 8

SIZE Up to 1 foot tall and 1½ foot wide

FLOWER COLOR White, pink, purple

SOIL Moist, well-drained

LIGHT NEEDS Full sun

ATTRACTS Bees, butterflies

Calendulas' flowers are edible, and they look beautiful in a summer salad; be sure to plant extras so you can share them with the bees!

Share some of this plant with your favorite indoor cat. Snip off a few sprigs and watch them munch on it.

Catmint
Nepeta

Gardeners love catmint for many reasons. For one, it's resilient. Also, once its purple blooms emerge, catmint will continue to flower for months, offering bees a steady source of nectar. Another plus: its silver-green leaves provide great color throughout the season, and emit a pleasant minty fragrance when you rub them together.

PLANT TYPE Perennial
HARDINESS Zones 3 to 8
SIZE Up to 3 feet tall and 4 feet wide
FLOWER COLOR Blue, purple
SOIL Well-drained, humus-rich
LIGHT NEEDS Full sun
ATTRACTS Bees, butterflies, hummingbirds

Celosia or cockscomb
Celosia argentea

Cockscomb's blooms look bushy, much like a squirrel's tail or a rooster's comb (which explains its common name). The erect, colorful, and feathery flowers appeal to bees and butterflies. This is a plant that tends to thrive in summer heat.

PLANT TYPE Annual for most areas
HARDINESS Zones 2 to 11
SIZE Up to 3 feet tall and 2 feet wide
FLOWER COLOR Orange, red, purple, yellow, pink
SOIL Moist, well-drained, humus-rich
LIGHT NEEDS Full sun
ATTRACTS Bees, birds, hummingbirds

Increase your chances of attracting bees with celosia by planting those with purple and yellow blooms.

Divide your chives every few years to keep them healthy and strong.

Chives

Allium schoenoprasum

Chives have so many benefits. Bees and butterflies go for the puffy, ball-shaped purple flowers. And you can eat the leaves, stems, and flowers; just mince them up to add flavor to soups, salads, sandwiches, and more. In addition, these plants often multiply from year to year.

PLANT TYPE Annual for most but perennial in some zones

HARDINESS Zones 3 to 8

SIZE Up to 2 feet tall and 1 foot wide

FLOWER COLOR Purple

SOIL Medium, well-drained

LIGHT NEEDS Full sun to part shade

ATTRACTS Bees, butterflies

Plant a line of crape myrtles on your front lawn or along your driveway to create both a stunning visual impact and a bee magnet.

Crape myrtle
Lagerstroemia

These southern charmers are staples in warmer climates and thrive in hot summers. There are dozens of varieties available, so you should be able to find the perfect plant for you. Bees rely on crape myrtles as steady sources of nectar throughout spring.

PLANT TYPE Perennial

HARDINESS Zones 6 to 9

SIZE Up to 15 feet tall and 12 feet wide

FLOWER COLOR Pink, red, lavender, white

SOIL Medium, well-drained

LIGHT NEEDS Full sun

ATTRACTS Bees, butterflies, hummingbirds

Crocus

Crocus

Crocus flowers give us hope that spring is coming. Though the flowers are just a few inches tall, their brilliant colors will brighten your still-drab garden and provide important sources of nectar to bees.

PLANT TYPE Perennial

HARDINESS Zones 3 to 8

SIZE Up to a few inches tall and wide

FLOWER COLOR Purple, white, yellow, blue, orange, pink, red

SOIL Average, well-drained

LIGHT NEEDS Full sun to part shade

ATTRACTS Bees, butterflies

Haven't had any luck with crocus? Try a different cultivar. Check with your local garden center for a recommendation. Plant the bulbs in fall.

Daffodils like sunshine in the morning, so think about this when you're planning where to plant them.

Daffodil

Narcissus

If you're a gardener who likes the philosophy of "more is better," you'll love applying this method to daffodils. When you plant these bulbs in fall, use lots of them to produce a gorgeous display in spring. Plus, the sea of flowers is like an "open" sign for bees. While other plants are just getting started, daffodils provide pollen and nectar for buzzing visitors.

PLANT TYPE Perennial

HARDINESS Zones 3 to 9

SIZE Up to 30 inches tall and 2 inches wide

FLOWER COLOR Yellow, white, orange

SOIL Medium to slightly acidic, well-drained

LIGHT NEEDS Full sun to part shade

ATTRACTS Bees, butterflies

Some gardeners love the challenge of over-wintering fuchsias indoors and trying to get them to rebloom in spring.

Fuchsia
Fuchsia

Gardeners with shady areas love these reliable flowers. Many people say fuchsias' complex, brightly colored blooms look like dancers gliding across the floor. (Once you see that image, it's kind of hard to unsee it.) You'll often find fuchsias in hanging baskets for sale in the spring. Blooms usually last through summer or early fall. Remember to water them regularly.

PLANT TYPE Annual for most

HARDINESS Perennial in zones 10 to 11

SIZE Up to 2 feet tall and wide

FLOWER COLOR Red, pink, white, violet, purple, bicolor

SOIL Medium, well-drained

LIGHT NEEDS Part shade to full shade

ATTRACTS Bees, butterflies, hummingbirds

Here's another good garden challenge: Try to cultivate globe thistles from seeds. If you can, collect the seeds in the fall and let them germinate in a cool, dry place during the winter. Plant them indoors in spring as you would other plants you're starting from seed. This will give them a strong start for transplanting to your garden once the chance of frost has passed.

Globe thistle

Echinops

This summer-blooming flower makes a bold statement in the garden, and with little maintenance. Like alliums, globe thistle flowers are ball-shaped. You can get gorgeous and unique cultivars of globe thistle, like 'Blue Glow,' 'Taplow Blue,' or 'Arctic Glow'. All are great for bees, so find the one that appeals to you!

PLANT TYPE Perennial

HARDINESS Zones 3 to 9

SIZE Up to 5 feet tall and several feet wide

FLOWER COLOR Blue, purple, white

SOIL Medium, well-drained

LIGHT NEEDS Full sun

ATTRACTS Bees, butterflies, hummingbirds

NATIVE PLANT TIP

This plant is native to much of California and parts of the West. Try to buy native varieties if you live in those areas.

Heliotrope tolerates shade, but it thrives in morning sun.

Heliotrope
Heliotropium arborescens

Heliotrope has been a favorite with gardeners for decades. With its brightly colored and aromatic blooms, it's perfect for containers, hanging baskets, and annual beds. It blooms outside for months, and many gardeners bring it indoors to overwinter.

PLANT TYPE Annual for most
HARDINESS Perennial in zones 10 to 11
SIZE Up to 2 feet tall and wide
FLOWER COLOR Purple
SOIL Moist, well-drained, organic
LIGHT NEEDS Full sun to part shade
ATTRACTS Bees, butterflies, hummingbirds

NATIVE PLANT TIP

Many hydrangeas are native to North America. Ask your local garden pro to help you find a native for your yard.

Hydrangeas vary in size. Larger varieties provide great shelter for butterflies, birds, and more. You might even get a hummingbird to nest in one!

Hydrangea
Hydrangea macrophylla

Some gardeners find it challenging to get hydrangeas established, but once they do, they're rewarded by reliable blooms for many years. There are dozens of hydrangeas on the market. They're available in two main types: those with globe-shaped flowers (mopheads) and those with flattened flower heads (lacecaps). If you keep them watered, both types will bring in the bees for many months.

PLANT TYPE Perennial

HARDINESS Zones 5 to 9

SIZE Up to 6 feet tall and 10 feet wide

FLOWER COLOR Blue, pink, purple, red, white

SOIL Acidic, well-drained

LIGHT NEEDS Full sun to part shade

ATTRACTS Bees, butterflies, hummingbirds, birds

Lamb's ear

Stachys byzantina

Once you discover lamb's ear, you'll always want it in your garden. It has beautiful, silver-green foliage that's soft and fuzzy and makes a nice ground cover in perennial beds. While it might not be big, tall, or showy, it's the perfect addition to any bee garden.

PLANT TYPE Perennial
HARDINESS Zones 4 to 8
SIZE Up to 1 foot tall and wide
FLOWER COLOR Purple, pink
SOIL Medium, well-drained
LIGHT NEEDS Full sun to part shade
ATTRACTS Bees, butterflies

Lamb's ear is known for tolerating dry and less-than-perfect soils, so if you have a challenging growing area in your yard, give it a try.

Lavender is a perennial, but it doesn't always have a long life; it often starts declining after a few years. To keep lavender going, add new plants every few years.

Lavender

Lavandula

Hands down, lavender is a favorite flower among the bees that live in the United States. Some gardeners say bees will travel a few miles from their hive just to taste lavender. This flower often peaks during what many gardeners call a "summer gap," when there are fewer flowers overall. It's rare to see a blooming lavender plant without bees all over it, so put it high on your list.

PLANT TYPE Perennial
HARDINESS Zones 5 to 9
SIZE Up to 3 feet tall and 4 feet wide
FLOWER COLOR Purple
SOIL Well-drained, alkaline
LIGHT NEEDS Full sun
ATTRACTS Bees, butterflies, hummingbirds

Lobelia
Lobelia erinus

Lobelia makes a great filler plant between perennials and annuals, both in the ground and in containers. There are many cultivars on the market, and each has its own benefits. Look for 'Laguna' for blue flowers, 'Lilac Fountain' for purple-pink blooms, and 'Rosamund' for red flowers.

PLANT TYPE Annual for most

HARDINESS Perennial in zones 10 to 11

SIZE Up to 1 foot tall and wide

FLOWER COLOR Blue, purple, white, red

SOIL Moist, well-drained

LIGHT NEEDS Full sun to part shade

ATTRACTS Bees, butterflies, hummingbirds

You don't have to deadhead this plant because it self-cleans and the blooms keep coming all summer.

Plant several shades of marigolds to increase visual interest and attract more butterflies and bees.

Marigold
Tagetes patula

There are many reasons why gardeners buy flats of marigolds in spring. They're one of the hardest-working and most resilient plants in the garden! They tolerate heat, drought, and even so-so soil, and they bloom for a long time. In addition to attracting bees, they also bring in other beneficial insects and deter some pests.

PLANT TYPE Annual for most

HARDINESS Zones 2 to 11

SIZE Up to 1 foot tall and 8 inches wide

FLOWER COLOR Yellow, orange, red, bicolor

SOIL Organic, well-drained

LIGHT NEEDS Full sun

ATTRACTS Bees, butterflies, hummingbirds

Many gardeners also love this plant because it's resistant to diseases and deer.

Marjoram
Origanum vulgare

Also known to many as oregano, this plant is a hidden gem when it comes to bees. Yes, you can plant it to eat yourself (just a few sprigs can go a long way on your pizza), but leave some to grow and flower for the bees, too. This plant does well in hot, dry climates, which many gardeners appreciate when they're planning a low-maintenance garden.

PLANT TYPE Perennial

HARDINESS Zones 4 to 8

SIZE Up to 3 feet tall and 2 feet wide

FLOWER COLOR Purple, white, purplish-pink

SOIL Average, well-drained

LIGHT NEEDS Full sun

ATTRACTS Bees, butterflies

Oriental poppy
Papaver orientale

Although poppies don't bloom very long, if you've ever seen their large, colorful flowers, you know why they're valuable in your garden. The blooms, which peak in mid- to late spring, definitely steal the show. Bees, butterflies, and hummingbirds will stop frequently for pollen and nectar. Poppies are easy to establish from seed, and likely will come back year after year.

PLANT TYPE Perennial

HARDINESS Zones 3 to 9

SIZE Up to 3 feet tall and 2 feet wide

FLOWER COLOR Orange, pink, red, purple

SOIL Medium, well-drained

LIGHT NEEDS Full sun

ATTRACTS Bees, butterflies, hummingbirds

While pansies are really popular in spring, they're also great to buy and grow in fall, which makes them perfect food sources for late-season bees and butterflies.

Pansy
Viola ×wittrockiana

Gardeners who are eager to get out in their gardens after a long winter love pansies because they're often one of the first flowers that appear in garden centers in spring. If you plant them as soon as possible, they'll provide ideal food sources for emerging bees. Pansies often bloom for several months, giving you a steady source of pollen and nectar, whether you're growing them in the ground or containers.

PLANT TYPE Annual for most

HARDINESS Zones 7 to 10

SIZE Up to 10 inches tall and 1 foot wide

FLOWER COLOR Red, orange, yellow, blue, violet, white, pink, bicolor

SOIL Medium, well-drained

LIGHT NEEDS Full sun to part shade

ATTRACTS Bees, butterflies

You don't have to do much to keep poppies going. They're even drought-tolerant, which can make gardening a little easier.

To encourage ongoing blooms, deadhead your phlox regularly to keep them beautiful and robust.

Phlox
Phlox paniculata

Garden phlox is a top performer in garden beds and is one of the longest blooming perennials you can grow. Once you get it established, it'll easily come back year after year, and will give you two to three months of color. Bees love it, and late-flying butterflies rely on its nectar.

PLANT TYPE Perennial

HARDINESS Zones 4 to 8

SIZE Up to 4 feet tall and 3 feet wide

FLOWER COLOR Pink, purple, red, coral, white, bicolor

SOIL Medium- to well-drained

LIGHT NEEDS Full sun to part shade

ATTRACTS Bees, butterflies, hummingbirds

Potentilla
Potentilla fruticosa

This shrub, also called cinquefoil, isn't very big, but it has many appealing traits. For instance, some varieties are hardy to zone 2, so it's one of the most cold-resilient shrubs. It also has beautiful, long-blooming flowers that give wildlife a steady and reliable source of food. Don't overlook this one because of its size. Tuck it in your perennial garden for years of great benefits.

PLANT TYPE Perennial

HARDINESS Zones 2 to 8

SIZE Up to 4 feet tall and wide

FLOWER COLOR Yellow, white, pink, orange, red

SOIL Medium, well-drained

LIGHT NEEDS Full sun to part shade

ATTRACTS Bees, butterflies, hummingbirds

This shrub can tolerate diverse soil types, including clay, alkaline, rocky, and dry, so if you have less-than-ideal soil, give it a try.

Grow sedums in groups of three or four to really bring in the bees and butterflies.

Sedum
Sedum

There are so many kinds of sedums! These perennials have thick stems and leaves, which reduce maintenance and boost drought tolerance. The clusters of tiny star-shaped blooms make a big impact in the garden in late summer and provide food for hard-working honeybees and butterflies. They often bloom through fall, providing rich colors for weeks or even months.

PLANT TYPE Perennial

HARDINESS Zones 4 to 9

SIZE Up to 3 feet tall and wide

FLOWER COLOR Pink, red, white, yellow

SOIL Medium, well-drained, slightly alkaline

LIGHT NEEDS Full sun

ATTRACTS Bees, butterflies

NATIVE PLANT TIP

Look for a sedum variety that is native to your area. *Sedum ternatum* is native to the eastern half of the United States, while *Sedum niveum* is native to the West.

This shrub continues to offer visual interest and cover in the fall and winter, which gives it four-season appeal.

Summersweet
Clethra alnifolia

Have a lot of shade in your yard? Summersweet, or sweet pepperbrush, is a good option because it will tolerate partial shade and even full shade if you have the right growing conditions. It produces beautiful, robust blooms in late summer, and its foliage turns bright yellow in fall.

PLANT TYPE Perennial

HARDINESS Zones 3 to 9

SIZE Up to 8 feet tall and 6 feet wide

FLOWER COLOR White, pink

SOIL Well-drained, slightly acidic

LIGHT NEEDS Full sun to full shade

ATTRACTS Bees, butterflies, hummingbirds, birds

Thyme loves full sun and a lot of heat, so plan accordingly before you plant it. If you grow it on a patio or deck, make sure it will get lots of light.

Thyme

Thymus vulgaris

Harvest thyme leaves for your own culinary needs, and then let it bud and flower to bring in bees, butterflies, and other nectar-seeking insects. This easy-to-grow plant often tolerates a wide range of soils, and you can grow it in the ground or containers.

PLANT TYPE Perennial
HARDINESS Zones 5 to 9
SIZE Up to 1 foot tall and wide
FLOWER COLOR Red, white, pink
SOIL Medium, well-drained
LIGHT NEEDS Full sun
ATTRACTS Bees, butterflies

Veronica also is a favorite source of nectar for butterflies from mid- to late summer.

NATIVE PLANT TIP

Veronica americana is native to much of North America.

Veronica

Veronica

The tall, spiky blooms of Veronica are quite striking. Since it often grows in one of bees' favorite colors (purple), it's easy to see why it's so popular with them in summer. This perennial is one of the few that produce a true blue bloom; look for cultivars like 'Crater Lake Blue' and 'Sunny Border Blue'.

PLANT TYPE Perennial
HARDINESS Zones 4 to 9
SIZE Up to 2 feet tall and wide
FLOWER COLOR Purple, blue, pink, white
SOIL Medium, well-drained
LIGHT NEEDS Full sun
ATTRACTS Bees, butterflies, hummingbirds

MORE NATIVE PLANT PICKS

It's always a good goal to grow native plants when you're trying to attract bees. Gardeners often want a list of plants that will be perfect for and native to their zip code, but it's not that straightforward. Some native plants can thrive in several areas or even most of North America. Organizations like the Xerces Society (*xerces.org*) have lists of native plants that appeal to pollinators, but your best bet is to find a local source of plants that are truly native to your region. Here are some additional native plant selections that grow in much of North America.

Swamp rose (*Rosa palustris*)

Black willow (*Salix nigra*)

Blanket flower (*Gaillardia aristata*)

Blue columbine (*Aquilegia coerulea*)

Common yarrow (*Achillea millefolium*)

Coneflower (*Echinacea angustifolia*)

Dotted blazing star (*Liatris punctata*)

False sunflower (*Heliopsis helianthoides*)

Heath aster (*Symphyotrichum ericoides*)

I Want to Bring in
BUTTERFLIES

Your garden can do so much good for butterflies if you plant the right flowers. Focus on these two key areas: host plants and nectar plants. To bring in the most traffic, it really is important to consider both. As a bonus, you can be sure that most of these plants also will be good for bees and hummingbirds.

In addition to planting flowers, there are other things you can do to make your yard friendly to butterflies. When you combine them, you're supporting butterflies and all wildlife. Here are some of the top things you can do.

Butterflies use their feet to taste, so it's important that all parts of the plant are free of synthetic pesticides.

Butterflies see colors in entirely different ways than we do. For instance, they can actually see ultraviolet light.

GO ORGANIC

When you make it a priority to use organic practices in your garden, all wildlife benefits. This means choosing pesticide-free garden products and organic alternatives when possible. You can do both big and small things to be more organic. For starters, make sure you're adding only certified organic matter and compost to your soil. You also can choose plants and seeds that are certified organic, which means they have been grown under approved conditions and haven't been treated with synthetic chemicals or pesticides. Once your plants get going, be sure to use only pesticide-free products. By doing these three things, you can feel good knowing that you've tried your best to make your garden safe for butterflies.

PLANT THE RIGHT COLORS

It's common knowledge that butterflies are attracted to purple flowers, but research has shown they also tend to favor white, pink, red, yellow, and orange. So as you can see, they're not all that picky!

PLANT TUBULAR FLOWERS

Like hummingbirds, butterflies are attracted to plants with tubular flowers. Butterflies have a long tongue, called a proboscis, that is often rolled up unless they're feeding. When they reach a flower, they unroll it and start drinking. Hummingbirds use their long bill and tongue to explore each bloom.

PLAN FOR LONG BLOOMERS

Butterflies rely on blooming plants throughout their breeding season. In early spring, when migratory species arrive and those that spent the winter locally emerge, they're hungry for the nectar of the first flowers, which aren't always easy to find. When they lay their eggs, their need for continuous food sources intensifies, since many butterflies have two or three broods per season. As the summer season fades, butterflies that migrate south for the winter need to stock up on nectar. Help them survive and even thrive by providing the food they need. By doing so, you'll get to enjoy them year after year.

OFFER A RESTING SPOT

Like all backyard wildlife, including birds, hummingbirds, and other insects, butterflies need safe places to rest. For this, they often choose flowering shrubs, so be sure to plant many of them in your garden. In addition, butterflies will rest near muddy areas that provide water and a cool haven. Mud can actually be good!

INCLUDE PLENTY OF HOST PLANTS

Butterfly caterpillars rely on host plants to provide the food they need to make a chrysalis and keep their life cycle going. Unfortunately, these host plants don't always have the flashiest or brightest blooms, so many people don't think of including them in their butterfly garden. In this section, you'll learn about some of the most common butterflies you might find in your backyard and the host plants each needs.

Butterflies often lay their eggs on the undersides of the host plants' leaves.

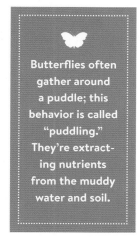

Butterflies often gather around a puddle; this behavior is called "puddling." They're extracting nutrients from the muddy water and soil.

Butterflies aren't able to fly during extremely cold weather. In fact, they fly best when the air is at least 80°F.

SOAK UP THE SUN

Butterflies thrive in sunshine and will be drawn to the flowers, shrubs, and trees in your yard if it's sunny for at least part of the day. That's also true for the pots and hanging baskets on your patio, deck, or porch. Remember this when you plan your garden.

Discover Common Backyard Butterflies

When you plant a garden with butterflies in mind, you could be rewarded with visits from dozens of colorful species. Here are some of the most common types you might see zipping in and out of your yard. They often move fast, so look closely if you'd like to identify them. »

Want to know how to tell the American lady from the painted lady? The American lady has two distinct eyespots on its hind wings while the painted lady has four.

American lady

Vanessa virginiensis

Here's another butterfly you'll often see flying around backyards and butterfly gardens. The American lady looks much like the painted lady, and it's a good challenge to learn to tell the two apart. These butterflies often migrate to warmer climates for the winter.

WINGSPAN Up to 2⅝ inches

MARKINGS Brown, yellow, orange, black; eyespots along the hind wing

HABITAT Gardens, meadows, open areas

RANGE Most of North America except the Pacific Northwest

CATERPILLAR Black bodies, red-and-white spots, black-and-green stripes

HOST PLANT Sweet everlasting, pearly everlasting, edelweiss, artemisia, ironweed, burdock

Black swallowtail
Papilio polyxenes

This swallowtail is also common in backyards across the United States. It's even the state butterfly of Oklahoma! It often stops in gardens that contain dill, which is one of its host plants. It prefers to lay its eggs on this common garden herb.

●▼●▼●▼●▼●▼●▼●

WINGSPAN Up to 4½ inches
MARKINGS Black with two rows of yellow dots along the bottom
HABITAT Gardens, fields, open areas
RANGE United States except the Pacific Northwest
CATERPILLAR Green with black bands, yellow dots
HOST PLANT Carrot, dill, parsley, Queen Anne's lace

These butterflies usually have two or three broods in a single season.

Bronze copper
Lycaena hyllus

It's often easy to get a good picture of this butterfly because it'll perch on flowers while it sips nectar. It's another butterfly that can be common in the North, so even those in cooler climates can see and appreciate this beauty.

●▼●▼●▼●▼●▼●▼●

WINGSPAN Up to 1⅜ inches
MARKINGS Males: dark brown with a purple sheen; females: bright orange forewings; both have gray hind wings with orange dots along the edges
HABITAT Swamps, streams, other areas near water
RANGE Northeastern United States
CATERPILLAR Bright yellow-green, with dark line down the back
HOST PLANT Curly dock, knotweeds

Black swallowtail males and females have slightly different colorings. Males have large yellow spots and some blue along the edges of their wings, while females have smaller yellow dots and larger blue dots. Females also are larger than males.

Cabbage white
Pieris rapae

Depending on the season and location, cabbage whites can vary from bright white to cream or even pale yellow. Since they range throughout North America, they're easy to spot in gardens as they look for nectar.

Some veggie gardeners consider the cabbage white a pest because its caterpillar eats the tender leaves of garden favorites like bok choy, broccoli, cabbage, and kale. If you're worried about this, plant extra veggies or use row covers to keep them out.

WINGSPAN Up to 2 inches

MARKINGS White wings with dark tips; males have a single black spot on each wing while females have two

HABITAT Fields, gardens, near water

RANGE Throughout North America

CATERPILLAR Green with yellow stripe

HOST PLANT Cabbage, broccoli, collards, radish, pepper grass, nasturtium, mustards

Common buckeye
Junonia coenia

This butterfly is named for the large eyespots on its wings that look like the nuts of the buckeye tree. It's easy to recognize, even at a distance. The common buckeye tends to be drawn to yellow flowers, so try to plant some in your garden.

WINGSPAN Up to 2½ inches

MARKINGS Brown wings with striped orange-black-and-white edges, large black-and-tan eyespots with white rings

HABITAT Fields, meadows, backyards

RANGE Most of North America except the Pacific Northwest

CATERPILLAR Dark green or gray with orange-and-yellow markings

HOST PLANT Snapdragon, plantain, figwort, stonecrop, sedum

While many butterfly caterpillars feed in groups, the common buckeye tends to hang out and eat alone.

Eastern comma

Polygonia comma

This butterfly loves wooded areas and sometimes visits backyards. Try to find it when it's perched, so you can see the silvery-white comma hidden on the undersides of its wings.

WINGSPAN Up to 2½ inches

MARKINGS Brown forewings with black splotches, silver comma under hind wing

HABITAT Woodlands, near water

RANGE Eastern United States

CATERPILLAR Light green or brown with spines

HOST PLANT Elm, nettle

The upper sides of this butterfly's wings are often black in summer and orange in winter.

When the giant swallowtail caterpillar feels threatened, it displays a pair of orange horns and emits an offensive odor to deter predators.

Giant swallowtail

Papilio cresphontes

This swallowtail is easy to see and identify because it's the largest butterfly in North America. The caterpillar looks like lumpy, black-and-white bird poop, which is a defense mechanism to keep it safe from predators. This graceful butterfly seems to float in the backyard as it searches for nectar.

WINGSPAN Up to 6¼ inches

MARKINGS Black with large yellow bands and dashes, blue dots on each side

HABITAT Sunny and open areas, gardens, citrus groves

RANGE Eastern United States, including throughout the South

CATERPILLAR Brown and white

HOST PLANT Citrus, prickly ash, hopwood, rue

Milbert's tortoiseshell

Nymphalis milberti

It's not often that you find butterflies thriving in high-altitude, northern regions, but this one does. It's common throughout Canada and Alaska. When its wings are open, it displays two distinctive oval shapes along the top edge of the upper wing that look like cats' eyes.

WINGSPAN Up to 2 inches

MARKINGS Dark overall, bright orange and yellow on outer wings, light blue dots along edges

HABITAT Temperate areas and higher elevations

RANGE Northern United States

CATERPILLAR Black, spiny with white flecks, green-and-yellow stripe on each side

HOST PLANT Nettle

It's common to see dozens of Milbert's tortoiseshells one year and very few another year.

During migration, monarchs can travel 100 miles or more per day.

Monarch

Danaus plexippus

This is one of the most widespread and beloved butterflies in North America, and conservation groups all over the United States are trying to protect it. You may be able to help, by planting milkweed in your garden, because monarch caterpillars need this plant to survive. It also makes the monarch poisonous to predators. By establishing milkweed, you may have monarchs for years.

WINGSPAN Up to 4 inches

MARKINGS Orange wings with black striping, white specks

HABITAT Gardens, forests, open fields

RANGE Throughout North America

CATERPILLAR White with black-and-yellow stripes

HOST PLANT Milkweed

Mourning Cloak
Nymphalis antiopa

This butterfly is one of the first to emerge in spring. You'll often find it perched and soaking up the sun. When its wings are closed, you might miss it because it can blend in with its surroundings.

WINGSPAN Up to 3½ inches

MARKINGS Dark brown or maroon wings with cream edges below a row of bright blue dots

HABITAT Parks, woodlands, backyards

RANGE Throughout North America but not in many Gulf states, including Florida

CATERPILLAR Black with white specks

HOST PLANT Elm, willow, aspen, birch, hackberry

Mourning cloaks are members of the brush-footed butterfly family. The name is descriptive; their front legs are small, hairy, and brush-like.

Orange sulphur
Colias eurytheme

You'll often recognize this butterfly by its flight habit, which is erratic and low to the ground. Some people know this as the alfalfa butterfly because of its affection for alfalfa plants.

WINGSPAN Up to 2⅜ inches

MARKINGS Yellow with a few orange or dark spots on wings

HABITAT Fields, prairies, backyards, other open areas

RANGE Across North America

CATERPILLAR Green with white stripes

HOST PLANT Legumes, alfalfa, clover, vetch, senna

While most people think of thistles as weeds, they're very appealing to the painted lady.

Females sometimes look white or green.

Painted lady
Vanessa cardui

This is one of the world's most widely distributed butterflies, found on every continent except Australia and Antarctica. It loves sunshine. On cloudy days, you might find it close to the ground or gathered around a puddle with other butterflies.

WINGSPAN Up to 2½ inches

MARKINGS Orange wings with white-and-black markings

HABITAT Backyards, forests, meadows, open areas

RANGE Throughout North America

CATERPILLAR Dark with yellow stripe

HOST PLANT Thistle family

When it's perched, look for the distinctive knobs on the ends of the male's antennae.

Queen
Danaus gilippus

You might mistake this butterfly for a monarch because its markings are very similar, it's attracted to the same host plant (milkweed), and it has similar habits. But look more closely and you'll see that, although its underside resembles a monarch's, the top side of its body is darker.

WINGSPAN Up to 3½ inches

MARKINGS Similar to monarch but deeper orange or orange-brown overall

HABITAT Open areas with milkweed

RANGE Most of North America, except northern areas

CATERPILLAR Black, white bands with yellow sides

HOST PLANT Milkweed

Want to know if you're looking at a male or female queen butterfly? Males have extra black spots on their hind wings. By the way, this also is true for male monarchs.

Pearl crescent
Phyciodes tharos

Native asters are this butterfly's host plants. They also bring in birds, hummingbirds, and bees. The pearl crescent is abundant throughout the eastern United States.

WINGSPAN Up to 1½ inches

MARKINGS Golden orange wings with dark undersides and pearly edges

HABITAT Fields, meadows, gardens, roadsides, other open spaces

RANGE Much of North America

CATERPILLAR Brown with black head and white or yellow stripe

HOST PLANT Aster

The pupa of this butterfly is brown, so it can be hard to see in the wooded areas where you'll usually find it.

Question mark
Polygonia interrogationis

Here's another butterfly that often hangs out in wooded areas and will wander into backyards. It looks and behaves much like the eastern comma. However, when it's perched, try to observe the undersides of its wings. Do you see a silvery question mark? It's fun to learn how to look for and recognize this.

WINGSPAN Up to 2⅝ inches

MARKINGS Orange-and-brown wings with a unique question mark on undersides

HABITAT Open woods, fields, roadside, streams

RANGE Eastern United States

CATERPILLAR Black body with white dots, yellow lines, orange spines

HOST PLANT Nettle, hops, hackberry, elm

If you put overripe fruit in a dish or feeder in your garden, you might attract red admirals to feed.

Red admiral
Vanessa atalanta

This medium-sized butterfly often stops in backyards in search of nectar. It's also considered a friendly butterfly and often perches on humans.

WINGSPAN Up to 2¼ inches

MARKINGS Dark overall, orange bars across upper wing and edge of lower wing, white-and-black spots on tips of upper wings

HABITAT Backyards, parks, forests, near water

RANGE Most of North America

CATERPILLAR White, olive, greenish-yellow

HOST PLANT Birch, poplar, willow, black cherry, hawthorn

Silver-spotted skipper
Epargyreus clarus

This is probably the most common of the many skippers that inhabit North America. You can learn to recognize this small garden butterfly by its flight pattern, as it zips from one flower to the next. Although it might resemble a moth, it's definitely a butterfly.

WINGSPAN Up to 2⅝ inches

MARKINGS Brown body, golden spots on forewings, silvery patches underneath

HABITAT Woodlands, gardens, meadows, parks

RANGE Throughout much of the eastern United States and parts of the West

CATERPILLAR Yellow-and-green stripes with orange eyespots

HOST PLANT Legumes, locust, honey locust, false indigo, wisteria

This butterfly is named for the silvery spot on the undersides of its wings.

You can find this butterfly even in colder areas like Canada and Alaska. Look for it on flowers, soaking up the sun.

Spring azure
Celastrina ladon

The spring azure is one of the smallest butterflies in North America, but it's also one of the most striking. Depending on the angle of the light, the season, and the butterfly's gender (males are brighter), it might show you a stunning flash of blue. It's especially visible in spring, when its host plants, the dogwoods, are blooming.

WINGSPAN Up to 1¼ inches

MARKINGS Grayish-white but sometimes bright blue

HABITAT Fields, forests, roadsides, backyards

RANGE Most of North America

CATERPILLAR Cream, green, or brown

HOST PLANT Flowering dogwood

Tiger swallowtail
Papilio glaucus

The eastern tiger swallowtail is a favorite among gardeners throughout the United States and Canada. In fact, it's the state butterfly of Alabama, Delaware, Georgia, North Carolina, and South Carolina. Depending on the location, males and females can be yellow with black stripes (just like its namesake mammal), although females also can be mostly black.

WINGSPAN Up to 6½ inches

MARKINGS Black-and-yellow stripes that resemble a tiger

HABITAT Parks, woodlands, gardens

RANGE Eastern United States and parts of Canada

CATERPILLAR Dark green with distinctive eyespots

HOST PLANT Ash, aspen, basswood, birch, cherry, cottonwood, tulip, willow

The western swallowtail resembles the eastern variety but has a different scientific name (*Papilio rutulus*) and is concentrated in western North America.

Many fritillaries have similar dots and patterns, so if you learn to recognize one fritillary, you should be able to recognize others.

Viceroy
Limenitis archippus

Viceroys are considered mimics because they try to match the appearance and behavior of monarch butterflies as a form of protection. Therefore predators think they are poisonous like a monarch, and they won't eat them. You can distinguish a viceroy from a monarch by the way it flies: the monarch glides while the viceroys flap.

WINGSPAN Up to 3 inches
MARKINGS Similar to monarch, but with curving black line along bottom of wing
HABITAT Backyards, woodlands, near water
RANGE Much of eastern North America
CATERPILLAR Mottled, bumpy, with bristles behind head
HOST PLANT Willow, poplar, aspen, cherry, apple

Viceroys don't migrate; the caterpillars hibernate by rolling up into the leaves of a willow or poplar tree.

Variegated fritillary
Euptoieta claudia

There is a handful of butterflies in the fritillary group, and they look very similar. This one, the variegated fritillary, is one of the most common and widespread species throughout North America.

WINGSPAN Up to 2¼ inches
MARKINGS Rusty orange wings, dark zigzag lines and dots
HABITAT Gardens, grasslands, meadows, fields, other open areas
RANGE Much of North America, except the Pacific Northwest
CATERPILLAR Salmon-colored body with white stripes, little horns on head
HOST PLANT Passionflower, mayapple, flax, violets, pansies, stonecrop

You'll often see the male butterflies on the ground. They're engaging in a behavior called "puddling" to absorb minerals from the soil.

Zebra swallowtail
Eurytides marcellus

Take one look at a zebra swallowtail's bold black-and-white stripes and you'll understand how it got its name. When it's perched, you can see red striping on the undersides of its wings. It's another swallowtail that's easy to identify, thanks to its coloration, larger size, and the long, tail-like parts of its wings.

WINGSPAN Up to 3½ inches

MARKINGS Triangular wings with long tail, black-and-pale stripes, blue-and-red spots

HABITAT Woodlands, meadows, near water

RANGE Eastern United States

CATERPILLAR Black with yellow-and-white bands

HOST PLANT Pawpaws

BUTTERFLY PLANT RECOMMENDATIONS

It can be remarkably easy to bring butterflies into your yard. More than likely, as soon as you start incorporating flowers into your garden, they'll magically appear. You'll see even more if you add the butterflies' host plants!

NATIVE PLANT TIP

This perennial is native throughout the Midwest and Great Plains. Look for the cultivar blue giant hyssop at native plant sales. The leaves of the cultivar anise hyssop add hints of mint and licorice to salads.

Encourage new blooms by pinching off and deadheading faded ones.

Agastache
Agastache foeniculum

This genus of perennials is in the mint family. Their small, fuzzy flowers appeal to all nectar-loving animals. Use the leaves to make herbal teas or jellies, or dry them and make potpourri. Since this plant easily reseeds and spreads on its own, it can quickly fill a garden bed.

PLANT TYPE Perennial

HARDINESS Zones 4 to 8

SIZE Up to 4 feet tall and 3 feet wide

FLOWER COLOR Purple or lavender

SOIL Medium, well-drained

LIGHT NEEDS Full sun to part shade

ATTRACTS Butterflies, bees, hummingbirds

When summer heat begins to take over, cut these plants back by as much as half. This might help them revive in the fall.

Alyssum
Lobularia maritima

If you want an annual you can easily grow from seed, this is it. Start your seeds indoors or sprinkle them in garden beds or containers. An added plus: alyssums' tiny flowers smell great.

PLANT TYPE Annual in most areas
HARDINESS Zones 5 to 9
SIZE Up to 1 foot tall and wide
FLOWER COLOR White, pink, purple, peach
SOIL Medium, well-drained
LIGHT NEEDS Full sun to part shade
ATTRACTS Butterflies, bees, hummingbirds

Astilbe
Astilbe

Gardeners love astilbes because they tolerate shade and add bright colors to areas where other plants won't thrive and bloom. Butterflies are drawn to astilbes' colorful and fuzzy flowers. After the blooms die, the fern-like foliage will continue to add lots of interest to your garden.

PLANT TYPE Perennial
HARDINESS Zones 3 to 9
SIZE Up to 5 feet tall and 2 feet wide
FLOWER COLOR Pink, red, white
SOIL Well-drained, slightly acidic
LIGHT NEEDS Part sun to part shade
ATTRACTS Butterflies, bees, hummingbirds

Astilbes tolerate deep shade, but for the best blooms, plant them where they'll get dappled sunlight.

Blue flax

Linum perenne

Flax is one of the true secret gems of the gardening world. Once gardeners discover it, they plant it again and again. It's easy to grow from seed. Just sprinkle some seeds in an open area, and there's a good chance at least some will take. Although the blooms last for just one day, the plant produces flowers for several weeks.

PLANT TYPE Perennial
HARDINESS Zones 3 to 9
SIZE Up to 3 feet tall and wide
FLOWER COLOR Blue
SOIL Medium, well-drained
LIGHT NEEDS Full sun to part sun
ATTRACTS Butterflies, bees

> Deadhead flowers to encourage new growth. Alternatively, if you leave the faded flowers on the plant, they'll turn into dark seed pods. Many gardeners love the look of these pods and enjoy them throughout the winter.

Baptisia or blue wild indigo

Baptisia australis

Baptisia adds deep blue and purple tones to the garden. The plant will live for a long time, so let it get well established and it will reward you with many years of pea-like blooms. Baptisia even withstands dry or drought conditions.

PLANT TYPE Perennial
HARDINESS Zones 3 to 9
SIZE Up to 5 feet tall and 4 feet wide
FLOWER COLOR Blue, purple
SOIL Moist, well-drained
LIGHT NEEDS Full sun to part shade
ATTRACTS Butterflies, bees, hummingbirds

> With this one, abundance is powerful, so grow as much flax as possible in a single area. You can create a little wildflower paradise if you plan ahead.

This plant loves moist soil, so give it lots of water while you get it established. This is also why you'll often see this wildflower near swampy areas or rivers.

Bluebells

Mertensia virginica

You have to see these flowers in person to experience how rich and beautiful they are. The pale-pink buds open into deep-blue blooms. As added pluses, bluebells are very low-maintenance perennials that improve over time, and they do well in part to full shade.

PLANT TYPE Perennial

HARDINESS Zones 3 to 8

SIZE Up to 24 inches tall and wide

FLOWER COLOR Blue, purple

SOIL Moist, well-drained

LIGHT NEEDS Part sun to full shade

ATTRACTS Butterflies, bees, hummingbirds

Establish bluestar in full sun. Not only will it thrive, but it'll be drought-tolerant.

Bluestar
Amsonia hubrichtii

In 2011, bluestar earned the Perennial Plant Association's Plant of the Year honor. Its foliage is a big reason to grow it; its fuzzy green strands turn golden in fall. Its star-shaped blue flowers draw many butterflies and bees.

●●●●●●●

PLANT TYPE Perennial

HARDINESS Zones 4 to 9

SIZE Up to 3 feet tall and white

FLOWER COLOR Blue

SOIL Medium, well-drained

LIGHT NEEDS Full sun

ATTRACTS Butterflies, bees

NATIVE PLANT TIP

This flower is native throughout North America, especially in the Midwest. Plant it in groups, which is how it grows in the wild.

Butterfly weed
Asclepias tuberosa

This perennial is in the milkweed family, so plant it as a host plant for monarch butterflies. As its name implies, it also attracts many other kinds of butterflies. It produces a steady supply of nectar, which makes it a must for backyard gardens. In addition, because it's native to much of North America, it tolerates a wide range of soils.

This drought-tolerant perennial is perfect for anyone who has limited water. It really is the kind of flower you can plant and forget.

PLANT TYPE Perennial

HARDINESS Zones 3 to 9

SIZE Up to 3 feet tall and 2 feet wide

FLOWER COLOR Orange

SOIL Medium, well-drained

LIGHT NEEDS Full sun

ATTRACTS Butterflies, bees, hummingbirds

Camellia
Camellia

Want something that blooms while other plants are dormant? Try camellia. This perennial shrub can flower in late fall to early spring—and even in the middle of winter—and the rose-like flowers attract butterflies, bees, and hummingbirds.

PLANT TYPE Perennial

HARDINESS Zones 7 to 9

SIZE Up to 12 feet tall and 10 feet wide

FLOWER COLOR White, pink, red, purple, yellow

SOIL Organic, well-drained

LIGHT NEEDS Part shade

ATTRACTS Butterflies, bees, hummingbirds

Do you love camellias but don't live in the right climate for them? Try growing them in containers instead so you can move them indoors when temperatures start to drop.

If you want to keep your mums thriving, divide them every few years.

Daylily
Hemerocallis

With daylilies, you get both long-lasting foliage that fills in areas effectively, and great flowers. As the name indicates, each bloom lasts just one day, but the plants flower all season, which makes them some of the most reliable food sources for butterflies. With so many colors available, find one that appeals to you.

PLANT TYPE Perennial

HARDINESS Zones 3 to 9

SIZE Up to 3 feet tall and wide

FLOWER COLOR Almost every color except blue

SOIL Medium, well-drained

LIGHT NEEDS Full sun to part shade

ATTRACTS Butterflies, bees, hummingbirds

Chrysanthemum
Chrysanthemum ×morifolium

As other flowers fade in late summer and fall, you can count on chrysanthemums to bloom through the end of the season. If you live in their hardiness zones, you can grow them directly in the ground. Otherwise, plant them in containers and move them inside before winter arrives.

PLANT TYPE Perennial

HARDINESS Zones 5 to 9

SIZE Up to 3 feet tall and wide

FLOWER COLOR Orange, pink, purple, red, yellow, white

SOIL Moist, well-drained

LIGHT NEEDS Full sun to part shade

ATTRACTS Butterflies, bees, hummingbirds

Daylilies grow well in shade, are considered drought-tolerant, and need little maintenance.

Deadhead dianthus after the first blooms die to ensure that you'll get more flowers throughout the season.

Dianthus
Dianthus plumarius

Dianthus flowers are delicate, a bit fuzzy around the edges, and absolute magnets for butterflies. This perennial starts blooming in late spring, right as butterfly activity starts to peak. Plant it in an area that receives full sun and it will come back for many years.

PLANT TYPE Perennial

HARDINESS Zones 3 to 9

SIZE Up to 3 feet tall and 2 feet wide

FLOWER COLOR White, lilac, red, pink

SOIL Moist, well-drained

LIGHT NEEDS Full sun

ATTRACTS Butterflies, bees, hummingbirds

> If you want to have enough dill for the swallowtails, bees, and yourself, sow the seeds several times over the course of a few weeks. This will give you a steady supply.

Dill
Anethum graveolens

Dill might not be high on your have-to-grow list, but it should be. For one, it's a host plant for black swallowtails. It's also attractive to beneficial insects. And it's delicious in salads, soups, pickles, and much more. While it's not actually a perennial, it often reseeds itself from one year to the next.

PLANT TYPE Annual for most

HARDINESS Zones 3 to 7

SIZE Up to 5 feet tall and 3 feet wide

FLOWER COLOR Yellow

SOIL Medium, well-drained

LIGHT NEEDS Full sun

ATTRACTS Butterflies, bees

Floss flower
Ageratum houstonianum

When you see a live floss flower, you will probably decide you have to have it in your garden. Its fuzzy purple or blue blooms make it a butterfly favorite. Sow the seeds directly into the ground or look for annual packs at your garden center.

▼ ▼ ▼ ▼ ▼ ▼ ▼

PLANT TYPE Annual for most

HARDINESS Zones 2 to 11

SIZE Up to 3 feet tall and 2 feet wide

FLOWER COLOR Purple, blue

SOIL Moist, well-drained

LIGHT NEEDS Full sun to part shade

ATTRACTS Butterflies, bees, hummingbirds

Floss flower is perfect as a container plant. Create your own container "recipe" of blue and purple flowers to really bring in the butterflies.

Lantana is perfect in containers or hanging baskets and will entice butterflies to your deck or patio.

Lantana
Lantana camara

If you love a tropical look, lantana may perfect for you. The blooms, which often are multicolored, become brighter and deeper and even create an ombré effect as the season progresses. Plus, butterflies love their tubular flowers.

▼ ▼ ▼ ▼ ▼ ▼ ▼

PLANT TYPE Annual for most

HARDINESS Zones 7 and up

SIZE Up to 4 feet tall and 3 feet wide

FLOWER COLOR Red, orange, yellow, purple, white, pink, bicolor

SOIL Moist, well-drained

LIGHT NEEDS Full sun

ATTRACTS Butterflies, bees, hummingbirds

If you're trying to establish a lilac in your yard, consider planting it in fall instead of spring. Also, if you need to prune it, do so right after it blooms.

Mexican sunflower
Tithonia rotundifolia

Although Mexican sunflowers aren't in the sunflower family, they do resemble "real" sunflowers. These annuals are easy to grow from seed. They also thrive in hot conditions and will keep blooming even during the hottest days of summer, which is great for butterflies.

PLANT TYPE Annual in zones 2 to 8

HARDINESS Zones 9 to 11 where it's perennial

SIZE Up to 6 feet tall and 3 feet wide

FLOWER COLOR Orange, red

SOIL Moist, well-drained

LIGHT NEEDS Full sun

ATTRACTS Butterflies, bees, hummingbirds

Lilac
Syringa

If you live in the right zone, lilac is a shrub that will steal the show in spring. Its tiny, fragrant blooms produce good sources of nectar for butterflies. Even after the flowers fade, it provides excellent cover, shelter, and nesting opportunities.

PLANT TYPE Perennial

HARDINESS Zones 2 to 7

SIZE Up to 15 feet tall and 12 feet wide

FLOWER COLOR Purple, blue, pink, red, white, yellow

SOIL Medium, well-drained

LIGHT NEEDS Full sun to part sun

ATTRACTS Butterflies, bees, hummingbirds, birds

At the end of the season, cut off some flower heads and turn them upside down to dry. Over time, the little seeds will start to drop, and you can save them to plant next year or feed to the birds.

It used to be hard to find milkweed plants in garden centers, but it's gotten much easier. Check early because they sell quickly.

Milkweed
Asclepias syriaca

This perennial is a must if you want to help support and attract monarch butterflies. They need milkweed; it's the only host plant on which the females will lay their eggs, and whose leaves the caterpillars will eat. Milkweed also has prolific, nectar-rich blooms that attract all butterflies and bees.

PLANT TYPE Perennial
HARDINESS Zones 3 to 9
SIZE Up to 5 feet tall and 1 foot wide
FLOWER COLOR Pink, white
SOIL Medium, well-drained
LIGHT NEEDS Full sun
ATTRACTS Butterflies, bees

Grow nasturtiums in your veggie garden, and they'll snake around your plants and provide great added color, shade, and weed-deterring mulch. Also, the flowers and leaves are edible, so try adding them to your salads. The pickled green seeds taste like capers.

Nasturtium

Tropaeolum majus

Nasturtiums will grow and thrive all summer—with little help from you. You don't even really need to deadhead them because the flowers will fade, drop, and take care of themselves. If conditions are right, the seeds will sprout in the spring. Vining and climbing varieties often grow up and around fence posts and trellises.

PLANT TYPE Annual for zones 2 to 9

HARDINESS Zones 10 and 11 where it's perennial

SIZE Up to 10 feet fall and 3 feet wide

FLOWER COLOR Red, orange, pink, yellow, cream

SOIL Medium, well-drained

LIGHT NEEDS Full sun

ATTRACTS Butterflies, bees, hummingbirds

Pasque flower
Pulsatilla vulgaris

The name of this flower tells a story. *Pasque* is the old French word for Easter, which often is when this plant blooms. The silky, delicate, purple flower appears very early in spring, which is perfect for the first butterflies. It's a welcome sign of warmer days ahead.

PLANT TYPE Perennial

HARDINESS Zones 4 to 8

SIZE Up to 1 foot tall and wide

FLOWER COLOR Purple

SOIL Fertile, humus-rich, well-drained

LIGHT NEEDS Full sun to part shade

ATTRACTS Butterflies, bees

Passionflowers can be sensitive to cold weather, so consider putting yours in a pot and moving it indoors in winter.

Pasque flowers tend to thrive in cool, dry climates and can tolerate high elevations. They're also great in rock gardens.

Passionflower or passion vine
Passiflora

Here's another exotic-looking, tropical flower. Passionflowers' bold, complex blooms almost resemble jellyfish. This prolific perennial vine curls around posts, fences, trellises, and arbors. There are many varieties to choose from: for purple blooms, choose *Passiflora incarnata*; for blue, try *Passiflora caerulea*; and for red, try *Passiflora coccinea*.

PLANT TYPE Perennial

HARDINESS Zones 5 to 9

SIZE Up to 30 feet tall and 6 feet wide

FLOWER COLOR Purple, blue, pink, red, white

SOIL Medium, well-drained

LIGHT NEEDS Full sun to part shade

ATTRACTS Butterflies, bees, hummingbirds

Russian sage
Perovskia atriplicifolia

Many gardeners may not be familiar with this perennial, but once they see it, they often want to grow it. Russian sage earned the Perennial Plant of the Year in 1995, and for good reasons. It has few disease or insect problems, is drought-tolerant, does well in many kinds of soil, and flowers from early to midsummer and into fall.

PLANT TYPE Perennial
HARDINESS Zones 4 to 9
SIZE Up to 5 feet tall and 4 feet wide
FLOWER COLOR Purple, lavender, blue
SOIL Medium, well-drained
LIGHT NEEDS Full sun
ATTRACTS Butterflies, bees, hummingbirds

As the blooms start to fade, cut them back in summer to encourage another round of flowering in fall.

Pincushion
Scabiosa

Once you see this flower, its name will make a lot of sense to you. The blooms look like they have tiny pins poking out all around. Its fuzzy appearance and abundant blooms (up to 50 per plant) really appeal to butterflies, bees, and other insects.

PLANT TYPE Perennial
HARDINESS Zones 3 to 7
SIZE Up to 18 inches tall and wide
FLOWER COLOR White, pink, lavender, red, burgundy, cream
SOIL Moist, well-drained
LIGHT NEEDS Full sun
ATTRACTS Butterflies, bees

Because this plant produces a lot of flowers, it can tend to flop over. To address this, you may want to put it in the back of your flower bed, where it also can support other plants.

Sea holly or blue thistle

Eryngium planum

The odd, prickly sea holly blooms appeal to many gardeners. They add interesting and unique textures when planted with other perennials. Its taproots make it very drought-tolerant. Plus, it doesn't require lot of care or attention.

One reason gardeners love sea holly is that it has a reputation for appealing to butterflies and bees while deterring deer and rabbits. If you have to deal with those challenges, plant this one.

PLANT TYPE Perennial

HARDINESS Zones 5 to 9

SIZE Up to 3 feet tall and 2 feet wide

FLOWER COLOR Purple, blue, silver, white, green

SOIL Medium, well-drained

LIGHT NEEDS Full sun

ATTRACTS Butterflies, bees

Spicebush
Lindera benzoin

When you plant a garden with powerful shrubs, you'll naturally support many kinds of wildlife. This is definitely the case with spicebush. This early bloomer attracts bees and butterflies that emerge in spring. Later, it's a host plant for the spicebush swallowtail butterfly. Spicebush also provides shelter for all animals, including nesting birds.

PLANT TYPE Perennial
HARDINESS Zones 5 to 9
SIZE Up to 12 feet tall and wide
FLOWER COLOR Green, white, red
SOIL Medium, well-drained
LIGHT NEEDS Full sun to part shade
ATTRACTS Butterflies, bees, hummingbirds

Spirea actually does well with a good pruning. Experts recommend pruning it a couple of times a year to keep it thriving.

Spicebush also produces berries that you can eat or leave for the birds.

Spirea
Spiraea

This shrub is one of the most common in backyards and public gardens throughout the United States. There are dozens of types and sizes, so choose the one that works best in your yard. Some varieties can bloom from early summer through fall.

PLANT TYPE Perennial
HARDINESS Zones 3 to 8
SIZE Up to 10 feet tall and 8 feet wide
FLOWER COLOR Pink, red, white, yellow
SOIL Medium, well-drained
LIGHT NEEDS Full sun to part shade
ATTRACTS Butterflies, bees, hummingbirds, birds

Sweet pea
Lathyrus odoratus

These reliable but delicate blooms can be challenging to grow in really hot climates but they're favorites in cooler areas. They're also great for kids to start indoors and then transplant to a sunny spot when the danger of frost has passed. It's important to note that the pods aren't edible. Their long-lasting and fragrant blooms will attract butterflies all summer and into early fall and fill your home with special sweetness.

You can grow sweet peas as vines or in clumps. If you grow them as vines, give them a little more attention at first to train them to climb.

PLANT TYPE Annual for most

HARDINESS Zones 2 to 11

SIZE Up to 8 feet tall and 3 feet wide

FLOWER COLOR Most colors except yellow

SOIL Medium, well-drained

LIGHT NEEDS Full sun

ATTRACTS Butterflies, bees

NATIVE PLANT TIP

This perennial is native to much of North America. It's best to split or transplant it in the fall.

Turtlehead

Chelone obliqua

This native plant thrives in many backyard conditions, including shade or filtered sun. It grows fairly quickly and can bloom for several weeks. Turtlehead comes in a variety of types and colors, so check out the best native option for your area.

When you plant a turtlehead, water it regularly to ensure that it will come back strong year after year.

PLANT TYPE Perennial

HARDINESS Zones 5 to 9

SIZE Up to 3 feet tall and 2 feet wide

FLOWER COLOR Pink, purple, white

SOIL Moist, well-drained

LIGHT NEEDS Full sun to part shade

ATTRACTS Butterflies, bees

Verbena
Verbena

Verbenas are great investments. Just give them a sunny spot and they probably will bloom all season. Verbenas are available as perennials and annuals. Your local garden center may offer several kinds, sometimes in containers or hanging baskets. Most gardeners choose a resilient annual.

● ● ● ● ● ● ●

PLANT TYPE Annual for most
HARDINESS Zones 7 to 11
SIZE Up to 4 feet tall and 3 feet wide
FLOWER COLOR White, red, purple, pink, orange
SOIL Medium, well-drained
LIGHT NEEDS Full sun
ATTRACTS Butterflies, bees, hummingbirds

These violets grow low to the ground, so some people use them as a groundcover.

Verbena is one of your best bets if you want flowers that will thrive in heat. While others start to fade, they'll keep going strong.

Violet
Viola odorata

Violets deserve a special spot in your garden. They're some of the sweetest-smelling flowers you can grow—and you can eat their flowers and leaves in salads, desserts, and iced drinks. They're especially attractive to fritillary butterflies, which use them as host plants.

● ● ● ● ● ● ●

PLANT TYPE Perennial
HARDINESS Zones 4 to 9
SIZE Up to 6 inches tall and wide
FLOWER COLOR Purple, blue
SOIL Medium, well-drained
LIGHT NEEDS Full sun to part shade
ATTRACTS Butterflies, bees

I Want to Welcome
OTHER WILDLIFE

By planning a garden with birds, hummingbirds, bees, and butterflies in mind, you'll build a strong foundation to support other animals. This is powerful. When you create a more natural environment, your trees, shrubs, and perennials will benefit wildlife, too. To be most effective, you'll need to provide the big three: food, water, and shelter. Here's how to achieve success.

OFFER FOOD THROUGH YOUR PLANTS

To bring in wildlife, you have to provide the foods they need while being aware of possible downsides. It's not as easy as putting out feeders for birds and hummingbirds. If you choose inappropriately, you might attract animals you don't want in your yard, including some that can become pests or even hazards. Instead, it's safer and more natural to offer plants, preferably natives, that will provide seeds, nectar, and berries. This also will support a healthy supply of insects that will feed beneficial animals like bats and spiders.

ADD WATER WHEREVER POSSIBLE

Animals need water. Large ponds and water features are ideal, but if you don't have room for one of those, try to include a fountain, birdbath, or other options. Even a small solar-powered fountain that sits on top of the water in an outdoor container can attract animals. If you do add a water feature, be sure to clean it regularly and fill it with fresh water. By doing these simple but important steps, you'll help prevent the spread of diseases. It's easy to forget this, so put a reminder in your calendar and make it part of your routine.

ADD AND INCREASE SHELTER

With birds and bees, you can easily add shelter by putting out bird or bee houses and hives. With other animals, the best thing you can do is add plants. Focus on building up a strong foundation of trees and shrubs. If possible, choose those that provide year-round appeal, including flowers in spring, berries in summer and fall, and shelter pretty much year-round. It can take a while to get these established, but they really should be a top priority when you plan your garden. Keep building on this base every year.

SAY NO TO SYNTHETIC PESTICIDES

It's been said, but it's worth saying again: don't use synthetic pesticides in your yard if you want to support wildlife. Many people are unaware that even small amounts of the products they use to kill weeds and make their grass grow can have devastating and even deadly impacts on wildlife. It's important to use certified organic products instead. Read labels carefully before you buy these products, and apply them according to the directions. It might be challenging to find and use other methods that are better for wildlife, you, and the larger environment, but your dedication will reap many rewards for years to come.

LET PARTS OF YOUR YARD GO WILD

To bring in wild animals, be willing to be a little wild yourself. Let go of your images of a picture-perfect, manicured yard. Do you have a pile of wood, rocks, or leaves in the corner? Leave it, because it's perfect for toads, turtles, and others. Have a dead tree or stump? Don't remove it, because you'll provide exactly what many insects and woodpeckers need. Wildness begets wildness.

KEEP PESTS UNDER CONTROL

Unfortunately, when you do all of these things, you also might attract less-than-desirable wildlife, like voles that can tunnel under your favorite plants or pesky birds that chase out the native ones. If you do have trouble with pests, identify the problem, determine if you can live with it (see the next paragraph), and if necessary, deal with it right away so it doesn't become much worse. Don't use synthetic pesticides to get rid of unwanted animals or insects because these toxic products can harm the animals you'd like to encourage to come to your yard.

BE WILLING TO SHARE YOUR SPACE

Part of welcoming wildlife to your yard is simply being willing to share. For instance, you might not love having an opossum in your yard, but once you learn how many ticks it can eat in a single season (about 5,000!), you might be more willing to let it raise its babies under your deck or behind your shed. Before you go to great lengths to keep wild animals out of your yard, be open to learning about them and letting them stay. Please read the next section for more information.

Discover Common Backyard Wildlife

It's one thing to attract beautiful butterflies and magical hummingbirds to your garden. Most people love seeing them up close in their yard. It gets more complicated when you decide to create a landscape that will appeal to other types of wildlife. For instance, while many people don't really want animals like opossums or bats in their yard, these and other creatures can be incredibly beneficial.

Here are some of the other animals you can attract to your yard and how to do so. Within each group, you'll learn about different species to look for, and gardening tips to help you out. Think about giving some of them a chance in your backyard. You might discover that they're much more helpful and entertaining than you realize. »

I WANT TO ATTRACT
BATS

Bats bring a lot of benefits to our backyards. For starters, they're great for controlling insects, especially mosquitoes. In fact, one bat can eat more than 5,000 insects in a single night. In addition, bats play important roles by pollinating flowers and spreading seeds. These small mammals often come out right at dusk. If you want to see them, go outside when the sun is going down to see them swooping and diving for bugs.

SPECIES TO LOOK FOR There are more than 1,300 bat species around the world and almost 50 in the United States. The hoary bat, the most common, is found throughout North America. Others to look for include the lesser-nosed fruit bat, little brown bat, and Mexican free-tailed bat.

GARDENING TIPS Bats are attracted to fruit and nectar. To create a bat-friendly yard, try planting flowers that bloom at night, like evening primrose, moonflower, and datura.

OTHER TIPS Bats will roost in a bat house. Find one online or build your own, and then hang it high in a tree.

I WANT TO BRING IN
DRAGONFLIES

Dragonflies are some of the oldest living insects in the world; they've likely been here for more than 300 million years. These incredible fliers have two sets of wings, which allow them to move quickly in all directions and angles. Although they're not pollinators, they eat problem insects like mosquitoes, so be glad when you see these fliers in your garden.

SPECIES TO LOOK FOR There are more than 400 dragonfly species in the United States. It can be challenging to see dragonflies' colors or markings because they move so quickly, but you might get lucky and see them pause on a leaf, branch, or even a bench. Take a moment to study them. The most frequent visitors include the green darner and the eastern amberwing.

GARDENING TIPS To attract dragonflies, include pools, ponds, water features, birdbaths, and plants like water lilies in your yard. You also can plant a rain garden to support an ideal habitat.

I WANT TO WELCOME
SPIDERS

Spiders don't always get the most love, but you really do want them in your yard. Not only are most of them fairly harmless, but they help control insect pests like mosquitoes and wasps. In addition, hummingbirds use strands of spiderwebs to help bind their nests together and provide elastic support for their nestlings.

SPECIES TO LOOK FOR North America has more than 3,000 spider species. Across the United States, you usually can count on orb weaver spiders to build their beautiful, classic webs.

GARDENING TIPS If you want to encourage web-building spiders to live in your yard, include tall plants like sunflowers and corn.

I WANT TO WELCOME
BENEFICIAL INSECTS

Beneficial insects not only boost the overall health and wellness of your plants, but they also play a large part in keeping those not-so-good insects in check. Most of the time, you don't even realize they're there, but if you look closely under leaves and between plants, you'll probably see signs of their activity. To bring these insects in, focus on filling your garden with healthy, robust plants.

SPECIES TO LOOK FOR Some of the beneficial insects you want to see in your garden include the ladybug, praying mantis, ground beetle, and hoverfly. All will eat pesky insects like aphids and Japanese beetles.

GARDENING TIPS One of the best ways to attract beneficial insects is to have something blooming at all times. Choose plants that flower in early spring, fall, and even winter, especially those that have long bloom times, like yarrow and goldenrod.

I WANT TO WELCOME
SQUIRRELS

Some people love squirrels but others don't, in part because they can eat some—or even most—of the seed and suet you put in your bird feeders. If you want to have a squirrel-friendly yard but don't want to constantly protect your feeders, invest in a feeder with a baffle. This will stymie the squirrels so the birds will get the food, and you'll still get to watch the squirrels' entertaining antics.

SPECIES TO LOOK FOR There are dozens of squirrel species in the United States, including 24 ground squirrels and 22 different chipmunks. The most common are the eastern gray squirrel, western gray squirrel, eastern fox squirrel, and American red squirrel.

GARDENING TIPS Plant trees like ash, oak, and maple, which usually produce good nesting cavities. You also can plant trees and shrubs that bear foods squirrels like, including berries or nuts.

I WANT TO WELCOME AMPHIBIANS AND REPTILES

If you see amphibians and reptiles in your yard, you've made it friendly for all wildlife. It can be challenging to meet their specific needs for food, water, shelter, shade, sun, and more, especially if you're starting with a bare space. But be patient. Add the most important elements first and keep building. Your efforts will pay off when a turtle crawls over the dry leaves under your lilac or a lizard climbs up the side of your shed.

SPECIES TO LOOK FOR There are more than 100 lizard species in North America. Welcome them to your yard. You might be fortunate to see other amphibians and reptiles, including American toads, tree frogs, box turtles, and even nonvenomous snakes like the garter snakes that actually eat slugs, snails, and voles.

GARDENING TIPS To attract amphibians and reptiles, be sure to offer plenty of cover to emulate a natural environment. Let your yard go a little wild, and add plenty of shrubs.

I WANT TO WELCOME
EARTHWORMS

Gardeners know that good soil is the foundation of a vibrant yard. Earthworms enrich and aerate soil, so consider yourself fortunate if you already find lots of them in your garden. Try to add more every year.

SPECIES TO LOOK FOR There are more than 100 species of earthworms in the United States. They look fairly similar and almost all of them are good for your soil. Unfortunately, some introduced earthworm species that are invading parts of the United States are damaging forest ecosystems. Ask your local garden expert to identify any worms that concern you and how you can deal with them.

GARDENING TIPS Earthworms thrive in soils that are rich in organic matter and compost, so if you incorporate as much of these as you can, you'll watch the earthworm population grow. You also can raise your own earthworms using a simple and inexpensive process called vermiculture; it's very popular with home gardeners.

I WANT TO WELCOME
MOTHS

Some people don't like moths, probably because of invasive and destructive species like the gypsy moth. But moths are beautiful creatures, and you could spend hours observing different species on warm summer nights. Flip on that back porch light and see who shows up.

SPECIES TO LOOK FOR There are thousands— yes, thousands—of moth species in North America. Compare that to the hundreds of butterfly species. Some of the most colorful and appealing moths that appear in backyards in the United States include the luna, polyphemus, cecropia, and tiger.

GARDENING TIPS Some moths don't have mouthparts, so you won't see them feeding on flowers, but they do perch and rest on them. Moths that do feed on flowers prefer the same nectar-rich types that appeal to butterflies. Focus on night bloomers like yucca since most moths are nocturnal.

I WANT TO WELCOME OTHER
SMALL MAMMALS

As you build up your garden and start to see birds, butterflies, bees, and hummingbirds, then you'll probably start seeing other animals. Embrace this. Yes, these animals can sometimes get into your garden and do naughty things, like the rabbits that eat all your young plants, but it's a good sign if you see these wild creatures. You have a healthy yard and garden, and other animals are taking notice.

SPECIES TO LOOK FOR Some of the small mammals to look for in your yard include rabbits, opossums, raccoons, and foxes.

GARDENING TIPS To support small mammals, try to create little pockets of habitat. For instance, you might leave standing dead plants in your garden in fall; these can provide seeds, perches, and shelter for a host of living things. You also can create little piles of rocks or wood to offer protection. One of the best things you can do is offer the shelter of trees and shrubs.

MORE SHRUBS FOR YOUR GARDEN

Shrubs can work magic in the garden, and they're essential if you want to create a wildlife-friendly space. Shrubs can sometimes get overlooked because they might take a few years to mature, but the investment in time is worth it because the benefits will last for years. In addition to the shrubs mentioned elsewhere in this book, here are a few more proven favorites.

Gardeners love this shrub because it's known to be resistant to diseases.

Fothergilla
Fothergilla major

Fothergilla is native to the southeastern United States. Its fragrant, nectar-rich, and feathery white flowers bloom in spring and pull in the pollinators, and its fruit brings in the birds. Perhaps even more appealing to gardeners, its foliage turns stunning reds and yellows in the fall. Although it grows fairly slowly, it will attract wildlife for many years.

PLANT TYPE Perennial
HARDINESS Zones 4 to 8
SIZE Up to 10 feet tall and 9 feet wide
FLOWER COLOR White
SOIL Moist, well-drained, slightly acidic
LIGHT NEEDS Full sun to part shade
ATTRACTS Birds, butterflies, bees

Hibiscus or swamp rose mallow

Hibiscus moscheutos

This shrub is a stunner. Its impressive flowers can measure one foot across. Hibiscus also attracts insects, and therefore other wildlife. It tolerates a little shade but prefers full sun.

PLANT TYPE Perennial
HARDINESS Zones 5 to 9
SIZE Up to 7 feet tall and 4 feet wide
FLOWER COLOR White, pink
SOIL Medium to wet, well-drained
LIGHT NEEDS Full sun
ATTRACTS Birds, butterflies, bees

These shrubs will tolerate some shade, but they will bloom more profusely if you place them in full sun.

As the flowers start to fade, deadhead them to keep the shrub looking great.

Mock orange

Philadelphus coronarius

This shrub got its name because its blooms resemble those of the orange tree. Gardeners love mock orange for its sweet fragrance. It's also a favorite of nectar-seeking insects, particularly butterflies.

PLANT TYPE Perennial
HARDINESS Zones 4 to 8
SIZE Up to 12 feet tall and wide
FLOWER COLOR White
SOIL Slightly acidic, well-drained
LIGHT NEEDS Full sun to part shade
ATTRACTS Butterflies, bees

Pieris or andromeda
Pieris japonica

If you have hot summers without a lot of rain, this shrub is a good option for you. In fact, it doesn't do well in really moist soils. In spring, it presents cascades of pink or white flowers that resemble lily of the valley blooms and smell like lilacs.

PLANT TYPE Perennial

HARDINESS Zones 5 to 8

SIZE Up to 12 feet tall and 8 feet wide

FLOWER COLOR White, pink

SOIL Medium, well-drained

LIGHT NEEDS Full sun to part shade

ATTRACTS Bees, hummingbirds

This shrub has deep roots, so it's often one of the first ones to recover from a fire.

New Jersey tea
Ceanothus americanus

New Jersey tea is round and short, usually only a few feet tall. It's native throughout much of the United States. It's especially popular with hummingbirds and butterflies, and it's a host plant to some azure butterflies and the mottled dusky wing.

PLANT TYPE Perennial

HARDINESS Zones 4 to 8

SIZE Up to 4 feet tall and 5 feet wide

FLOWER COLOR White

SOIL Medium, well-drained

LIGHT NEEDS Full sun to part shade

ATTRACTS Birds, butterflies, hummingbirds

You may want to consider growing this shrub in containers on a deck or patio.

Pussy willows like lots of moisture, so it's important to keep them watered when you're getting them established in your garden.

Pussy willow
Salix discolor

This shrub can often look like a tree because it grows fast and tall. In early spring, its furry catkins look great and provide nectar for various pollinators. Prune this shrub regularly to maintain its appealing, compact shape.

PLANT TYPE Perennial
HARDINESS Zones 4 to 8
SIZE Up to 15 feet tall and 12 feet wide
FLOWER COLOR Yellowish-green
SOIL Moist, well-drained
LIGHT NEEDS Full sun to part shade
ATTRACTS Birds, butterflies, bees

Rugosa rose
Rosa rugosa

If you love roses but think traditional rosebushes are a little finicky, try rugosa rose. This easy-to-grow shrub tolerates many soil types and growing conditions. It also attracts pollinators during the summer blooming season, and then forms fruit called rose hips in late summer and fall that will bring in the birds. You can eat them, too. The hips are packed with vitamin C. Enjoy them dried in tea or made into jam or syrup. In some areas, it's considered aggressive, so be aware of this if you choose to add it to your garden.

PLANT TYPE Perennial
HARDINESS Zones 2 to 7
SIZE Up to 8 feet tall and 6 feet wide
FLOWER COLOR Pink, red, lavender, white
SOIL Rich, well-drained
LIGHT NEEDS Full sun to part shade
ATTRACTS Birds, hummingbirds, butterflies

These shrubs have thorns, so it's best to place them in the back of a perennial bed or against a fence.

Show Me How to
PLAN A GARDEN

It's fun to mix and match plants in the garden. As long as you pay attention to plants' light, water, and soil needs, you can try a variety of planting combos. When gardeners plan a new garden bed, they often like to start with a single plant they love and build around it. If you're starting with an existing garden, determine if you have enough space for the plants you want to add or if you need to remove something to make room.

With more than 100 plants to choose from in this book, you should have plenty of options to create your own garden plans. Here are some inspirations to get you started.

I Want to Plant a
HUMMINGBIRD GARDEN

This plan will fill your yard with blooms throughout the season.
Many of these flowers come in several colors.

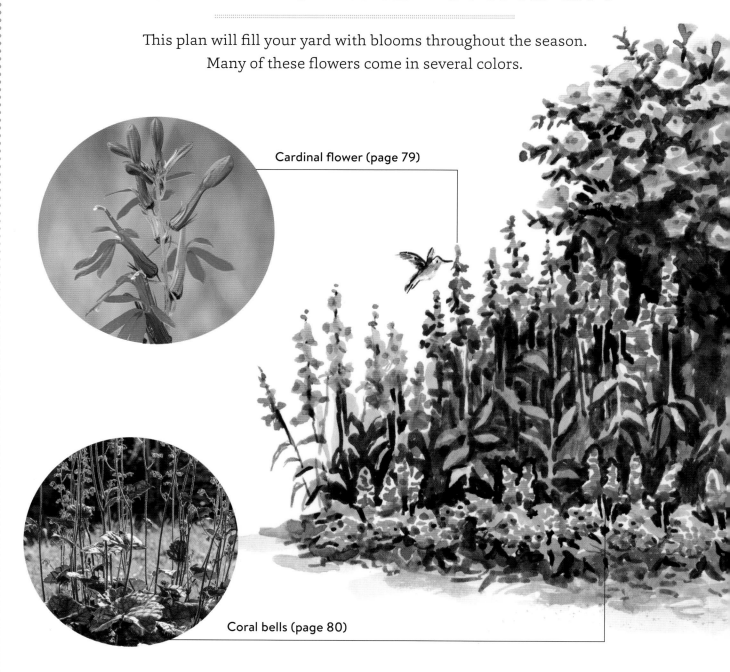

Cardinal flower (page 79)

Coral bells (page 80)

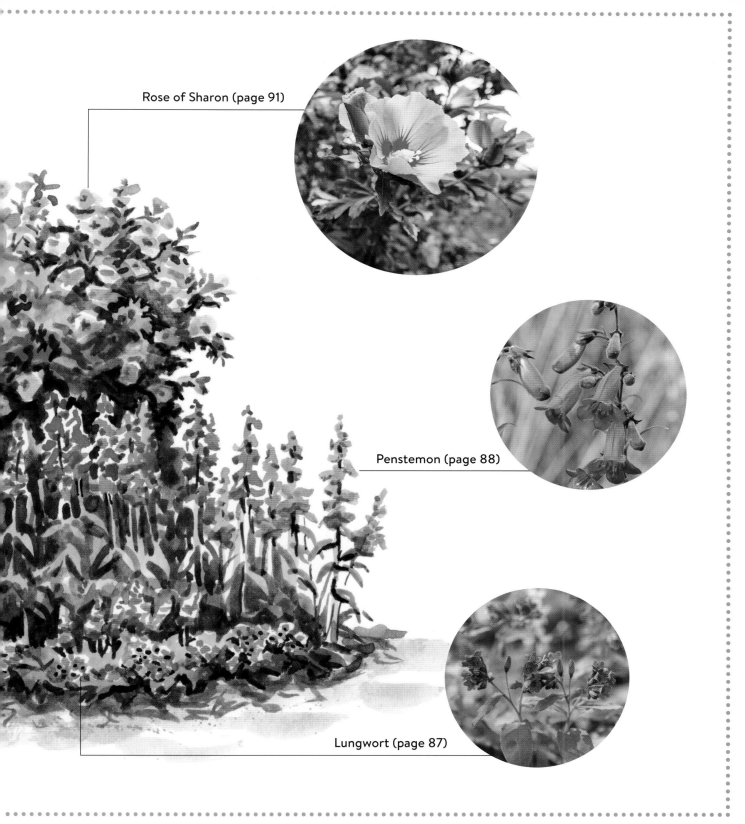

Rose of Sharon (page 91)

Penstemon (page 88)

Lungwort (page 87)

I Want to Plant a
SHADE GARDEN

Shade can be one of the toughest gardening challenges to tackle.
Here's a garden you can count on to bring in birds, bees, butterflies,
and more wildlife—even if you have a very shady spot.

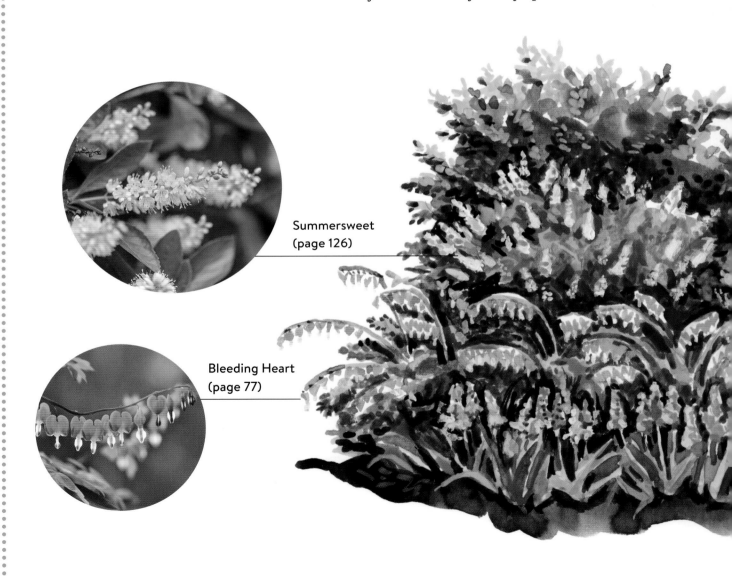

Summersweet
(page 126)

Bleeding Heart
(page 77)

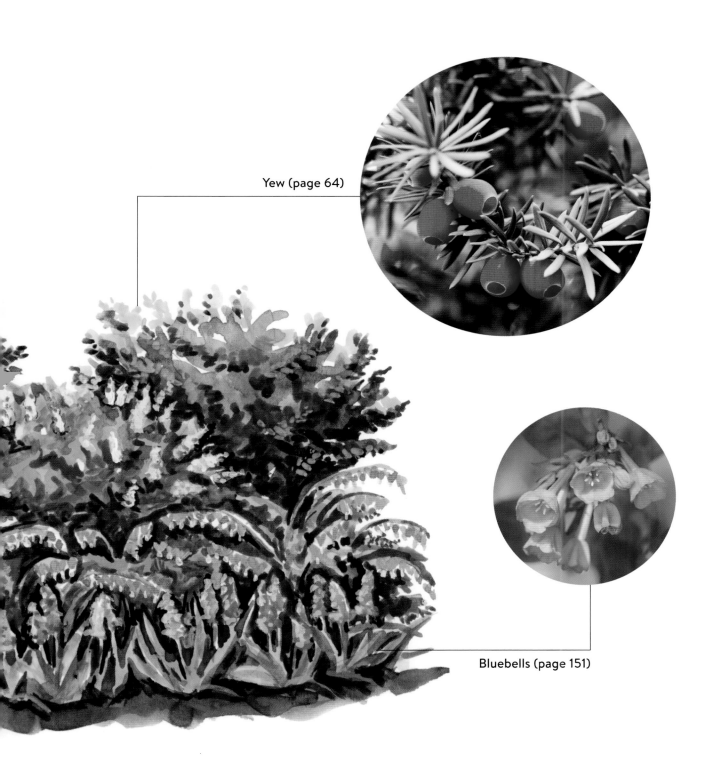

Yew (page 64)

Bluebells (page 151)

I Want to Plant a
SONGBIRD GARDEN

Birds—especially songbirds—are going to have plenty to eat
with this garden plan: nectar, berries, and lots of natural birdseed.
Plus, you'll get to enjoy the plants' flowers for many months.

Joe-pye weed
(page 56)

Purple coneflower (page 58)

Viburnum (page 62)

Fountain grass
(page 54)

Black-eyed Susan (page 46)

I Want to Plant a
BUTTERFLY GARDEN

This butterfly garden perfectly mixes nectar-producing host plants and flowers that bloom from spring into early fall. It's a great example of how to complement plants like dill and butterfly weed with other garden favorites.

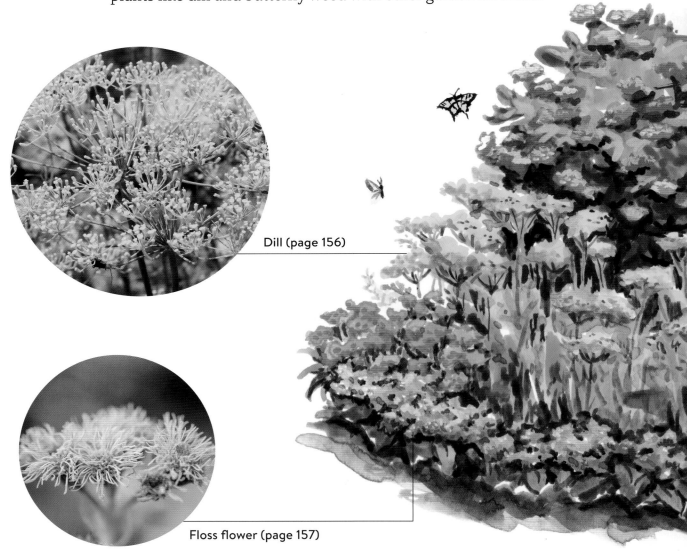

Dill (page 156)

Floss flower (page 157)

Spirea (page 164)

Butterfly weed
(page 152)

I Want to Plant a
DROUGHT-TOLERANT GARDEN

Here's a garden that you can plant and leave alone. Start with these four drought-tolerant garden staples and add more over the years.

Goldenrod
(page 55)

Coreopsis (page 49)

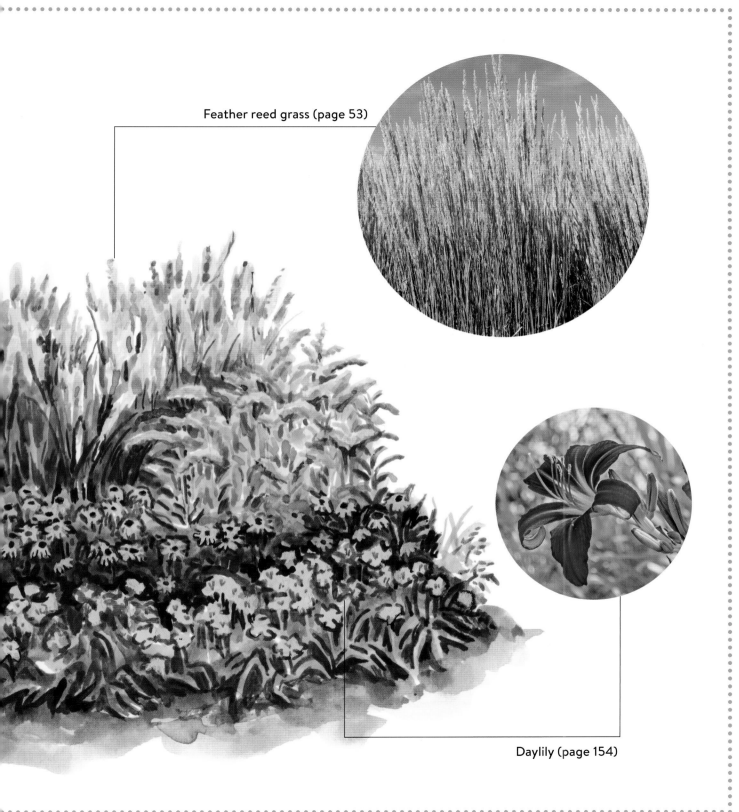

Feather reed grass (page 53)

Daylily (page 154)

I Want to Plant a
BIRDSEED GARDEN

You'll have an endless supply of seed for backyard birds when
you add these flowers. All of them bloom from summer through early fall.
Leave them up all winter so birds can eat their nourishing seeds.

Cosmos (page 50)

Purple coneflower (page 58)

Sunflower (page 61)

Black-eyed Susan
(page 46)

I Want to Plant a
BEE-FRIENDLY GARDEN

You'll bring in bees from early spring to late fall with these plants. Their staggered bloom times ensure steady supplies of nectar and pollen. Add to these excellent base plants and you'll turn your garden into a bee-friendly space.

Bee balm (page 108)

Chives (page 113)

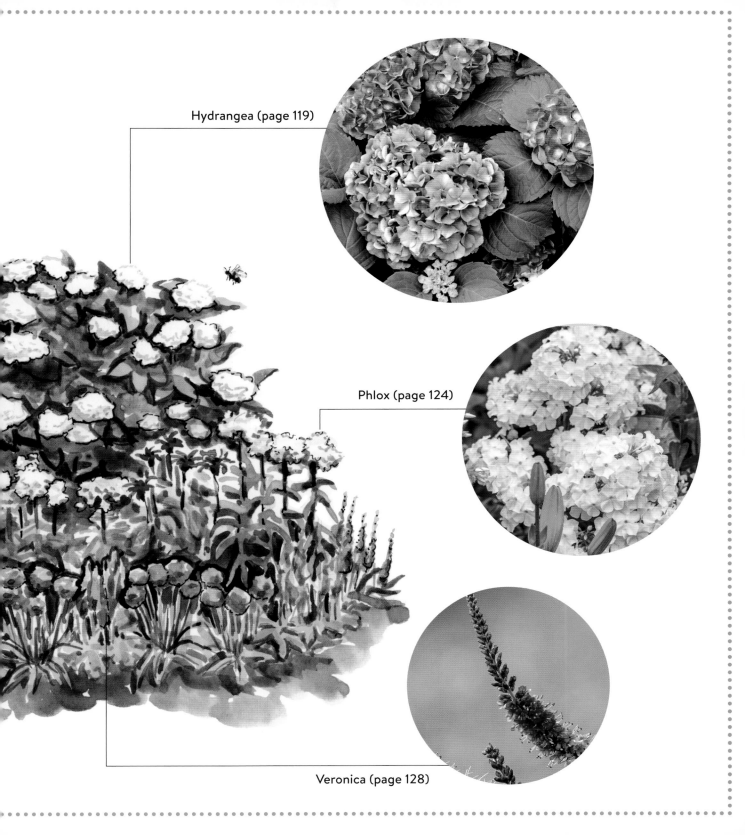

Hydrangea (page 119)

Phlox (page 124)

Veronica (page 128)

I Want to Plant a
NATIVE GARDEN

These native plants, found throughout North America,
will bring birds, bees, and butterflies to your garden.
Check for local varieties that are best suited to your location.

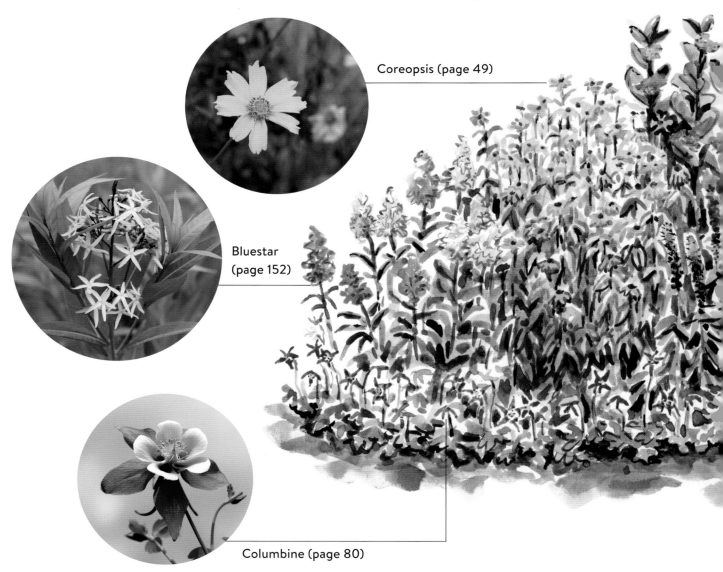

Coreopsis (page 49)

Bluestar (page 152)

Columbine (page 80)

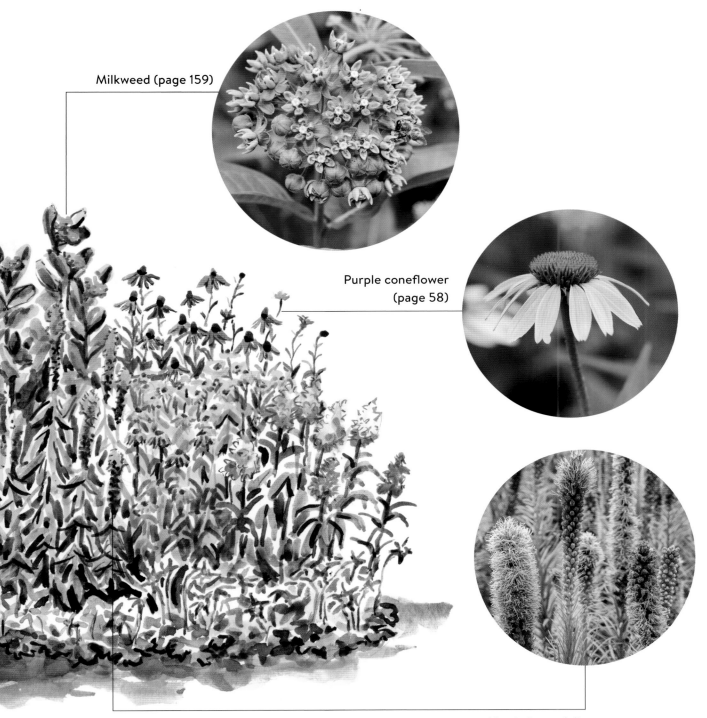

Milkweed (page 159)

Purple coneflower
(page 58)

Liatris (page 86)

I Want to Plant a
BIRD HABITAT GARDEN

If you want to create a habitat that draws birds,
it's always good to start with strong staples, such as these trees, shrubs,
and grasses. You can add perennials and annuals later.

Beautyberry (page 46)

Fountain grass (page 54)

Dogwood (page 52)

Elderberry
(page 53)

I Want to Plant a
LOW-MAINTENANCE GARDEN

These easy-care plants will bloom for years.

Cosmos (page 50)

Daylily (page 154)

Buttonbush (page 110)

Sedum (page 125)

FAQS

Organic Gardening

WHAT DOES IT MEAN TO HAVE
AN ORGANIC GARDEN?

When you garden organically, you don't use synthetic pesticides or fertil-izers. Instead, you use other practices and products to build healthy soil, nurture plants, and control pests and weeds. For instance, you'll need to add organic matter to improve your soil. But it's more than changing the prod-ucts you use. It's really about thinking of your garden holistically and going green in every way you can—from the seeds you buy to how you deal with pests. Organic practices will support your health and will benefit the health, and even survival, of the other living things in your garden. By adhering to natural practices, you're helping give bees, butterflies, birds, and other crea-tures the environment they seek.

WHY IS AN ORGANIC GARDEN IMPORTANT?

Most of us are unaware of the prevalence of nonorganic chemicals in our environment, including in the seeds we grow and the products we put on our grass. It might seem like man-made products can't do much harm, but some research suggests that organic gardens can have more than 50% more bird and insect activity (*Journal of Applied Ecology*). By switching to organic practices and products, you'll help wildlife.

HOW DO YOU BUILD ORGANIC SOIL?

This is one of the most important things you can do to improve your garden. You can't make high-quality organic soil overnight, but the good news is that it's relatively easy and effective to tackle yourself. If you have a small space, you can create your own compost from kitchen scraps and some yard debris fairly quickly. You also can try vermiculture: harnessing worms to turn your kitchen scraps into remarkable soil-building poop called castings. If you have a larger area, you might need to bring in compost from a local farm or other organic gardening source. If you go this route, it's really important to make sure that you're buying from a high-quality provider.

WHERE DO YOU FIND ORGANIC SEEDS OR PLANTS?

You can find several organic seed and plant options online, including on sites like Etsy. Also, search for organic farms and garden centers nearby. Contact members of a local gardening group and your state's agricultural extension service. Look for suppliers whose products are labeled "certified organic" which ensures that they were grown or processed without synthetic chemicals or pesticides.

HOW LONG DOES IT TAKE TO CREATE AN ORGANIC GARDEN?

It can take about three years to build organic soil, but you can start working on it immediately, by adding compost and eliminating synthetic chemicals and fertilizers. You also can switch to organic seeds and plants right away. Over time, you can replace your other garden practices and products with organic ones.

HOW CAN YOU CONTROL WEEDS IN AN ORGANIC GARDEN?

To start with, the best way to control weeds is to work to prevent them. You can do this by having healthy soil, adding compost, and using mulch to suppress weeds. If you still have weed problems, look for organic herbicides. There are far more of these products on the market today than there were ten years ago. If you can't find a good selection locally, buy online. You also can make your own organic weed controls. One of the most popular recipes consists of one gallon of vinegar, one cup of salt, and one tablespoon of dish soap. Mix it well and spray it on the weeds. There are many other recipes online, so try a few to see what works.

HOW CAN YOU CONTROL PESTS IN AN ORGANIC GARDEN?

If you're dealing with an infestation, you can apply organic pest-control products, including insecticidal soap and neem-oil. Both are proven effective for dealing with certain pests. Many garden centers sell a variety of organic options. But the most effective, and long-lasting, way to deal with pests is by creating a vibrant garden built on healthy soil. This includes attracting beneficial insects and wildlife. Many good bugs will take care of the bad ones.

IS GROWING ORGANIC EXPENSIVE OR HARD?

At first, it might seem a little expensive to switch to organic gardening. Seeds, plants, and other organic supplies tend to cost more than nonorganic. Over time, your investment now will pay off later because you'll need to buy fewer inputs. Also, you can find a lot of inexpensive or free homemade remedies and options for going organic; you don't have to buy fancy products in order to lead a more organic life. Start small and you'll likely find it's a lot easier and more affordable than you think.

Growing Natives

WHAT DOES IT MEAN TO GROW NATIVE PLANTS?

Native plants are those you would have found naturally in an area hundreds or even thousands of years ago. Nobody planted them there. Native plants tend to have many natural benefits, especially for birds, bees, and other wildlife. Over the years, people have planted nonnative plants for a variety of reasons, including providing food, creating beauty, and controlling pests. They might also have bought a nonnative plant unknowingly. While the prevalence of nonnative plants has increased the variety of appealing options for your garden, it's also created some challenges. This doesn't mean that all nonnative plants are bad for the environment. However, by focusing on natives and making an effort to plant more of them in your garden, you might help restore some of the natural habitats we've lost. Plus, when you ask for native plants at your local gardening store, they might start offering more of them.

ARE NATIVE PLANTS BETTER THAN NEWER VARIETIES?

If you're planting for pollinators, then yes, natives are better overall. Studies have shown that the more we manipulate plants and breed them to be beneficial for other reasons, such as longer bloom times and more flowers in a greater range of colors, the less beneficial they are to pollinators. It can be tempting to choose new cultivars that promise unique colors, double blooms, or other benefits, but if you're planning a garden for bees, butterflies, and others, natives are often your best choice. If you plant new cultivars, research them to ensure they're attractive to pollinators.

DOES MY REGION HAVE DIFFERENT NATIVES THAN ANOTHER REGION?

Yes, no, and maybe. There are many plants that are native to your region. After all, growing conditions from Oregon to Wisconsin and Florida differ a lot. But the truth is, there's a lot of crossover range with natives; some are indigenous from coast to coast. Remember this as you plan your garden. Yes, it's good to keep natives in mind, but that doesn't necessarily mean you should limit yourself to specific plants that are available only in your city, state, or region. Don't shy away from plants at "regular" garden centers and stores, even if they're not labeled "native." They may be great for your garden, and they might even be natives.

WHAT'S THE BEST WAY TO GET RECOMMENDATIONS OF NATIVE PLANTS THAT MIGHT DO WELL IN MY GARDEN?

To start with, you'll find a lot of great suggestions by searching online for "native plants" and adding the name of your state or region. You might find a local native plant society or other organizations dedicated to preserving native plants in your area. You also might search Facebook for groups and individuals near you who are growing native plants. And check with your local library or nature center for helpful books, magazines, or other resources. Even older books will likely provide useful information, because if a plant was native 20 years ago, it's still native today.

WHY CAN'T I FIND MORE NATIVE PLANTS FOR MY AREA?

Gardeners often look for recommendations that are specific to their region—or even their backyard—but you might not find that information, except in a resource written for your area. If a plant isn't described as native to your area, that doesn't mean it's not, or that it won't be appropriate in your yard. Remember that numerous plants are native to many areas of North America. For instance, what's native to New Jersey also could be native to Illinois or Idaho. Remember this as you read lists of native plants and you'll probably find many more options than you thought you'd have.

HOW DO NATIVE PLANTS HELP BIODIVERSITY?

The term *biodiversity* refers to the many types of things that live in an area and their complex and interconnected relationships. Stronger diversity is better. Native plants have adapted to their surroundings while providing numerous benefits, including food and shelter for animals, and helping build soil.

WHERE DO I BUY NATIVE PLANTS?

Just like other plants, you can buy natives locally or online. If you buy online, make sure the source is located in your area or provides plants grown for your conditions. Ask local gardeners, members of your native plant society or local gardening groups, and others for their recommendations and information about native plant sales and other helpful resources.

Common Garden Challenges

HOW DO I DEAL WITH WEEDS THAT TAKE OVER MY GARDEN?

As you switch to a more organic way of gardening, you might have more weeds at first. It might be tempting to reach for the weed-control products you know will work right away, but try to resist. Stick with organic practices and products. It might take some extra effort to keep weeds under control by digging them up and mulching them, but over time you'll reduce the weed population. It's worth it in the long term.

WHAT DO I DO WHEN PLANTS ARE AGGRESSIVE?

As you switch to organic products, you might notice that some plants become aggressive and can take over flower beds or whole gardens. The best way to deal with them is to remove them right away. Search online to see if a specific plant is known for spreading all over a garden and if so, how to remove or contain it in a pot or a bed with sturdy borders.

HOW DO I BUILD UP A GARDEN QUICKLY?

Many gardeners want to know how to use fast-growing plants to turn a blank or bare space into a garden that supports birds, bees, and other wildlife. If this is the case for you, here are some options. First, look for plants that are known to grow rapidly. Check the plant descriptions and labels carefully. Be patient while the plants take the time they need to spread. The other option is to look for mature plants from local tree companies and nurseries. You'll probably pay more for them, but they'll give you the results you want in much less time.

WHAT IF I CAN'T GET PLANTS TO GROW IN CERTAIN AREAS?

Everyone has tough gardening spaces that might have poor soil, little sun, or other challenges. If this is the case for you, don't give up. First, you'll need to understand the problem. For instance, if you have less-than-ideal soil, work at amending it. If you're dealing with drought or shade issues, focus on plants that thrive under these conditions. Remember that you're not the only one who has faced these challenges, so do your research and you'll find many helpful resources.

HOW DO I DEAL WITH POOR SOIL?

Do you know you have poor soil, or just suspect it? To find out, get your soil tested. You can buy simple soil-testing kits online that will give you a start, but it's better to get more detailed information, either by buying a more sophisticated test or by hiring a local or state expert to test your soil for you. In some areas, you can get these tests for free.

HOW DO I DIAGNOSE A GARDEN PROBLEM?

Many times, there are signs of a potential garden problem before it's in full force. If you notice your plants are wilting or discolored, have spots or holes on their leaves, or show other signs of distress, take lots of pictures of them. This will help you diagnose what's going on. Share your photos or plant samples with a gardener friend or the staff at your local garden center. You also can look for apps that will connect you to experts online. Do the same for garden problems that aren't directly related to the plant, such as signs that voles are causing the damage.

WHY CAN'T I GET A CERTAIN PLANT ESTABLISHED?

Here's a scenario: You've tried to grow hydrangeas but can't get them established no matter what you do. That can be frustrating, but you don't have to give up. First, you must determine if the area you've chosen actually provides the conditions hydrangeas need. Many gardeners want a certain plant so much they forget to read the labels or research its needs—for instance, trying to grow a plant that requires full sun in an area of full shade. If you've verified that the area you're planting in is a good fit, then check your soil. You may have to amend it to meet the plant's requirements. There are many other reasons a plant might have trouble getting established—like being hit by a late cold snap or being planted at the wrong time of year—but if you've chosen an appropriate variety, put it in the optimal place, and given it what it needs, try again. If it's not a good fit, choose another plant. There are so many good options.

Other

WHY CAN'T I ATTRACT HUMMINGBIRDS?

Hummingbirds are one of the most sought-after birds in North America. There's a good chance you have hummingbirds in your area but they're so small and move so fast that you might not know they're around. They aren't hard to attract, but it may take some time for them to find your garden. One of the easiest ways to bring them in is to put up sugar-water hummingbird feeders early in the season. You can contact your local bird-watching organization or search online or in bird and garden books and magazines to determine when hummingbirds usually arrive in your area. If you put out feeders when hummingbirds first arrive and begin establishing their territories, they're more likely to visit your yard for months. If you miss this opportunity and don't see hummingbirds right away, try again in late summer, when they start preparing to fly south for the winter. You'll increase your odds of attracting them into your garden—this year and perhaps for many years to come.

WHERE ARE ALL THE BUTTERFLIES AND BEES?

This is another case where they might be there but you just have to know where and when to look. Both butterflies and bees prefer warm, sunny days, so that's when to watch for them in your garden. If you don't see any, determine if you have the kinds of plants that appeal to these pollinators. It may take time to get these plants established, but stick with it and you'll enjoy the rewards.

HOW DO I KNOW WHICH PLANTS TO GROUP TOGETHER?

This can be challenging. First, always read the labels on the seeds and plants you want to buy. Pay attention to their requirements for light and water, the soil types they prefer, and how large they'll be when mature. By grouping plants with similar needs, you'll be more likely to create a robust garden. For inspiration, check out the planting plans (starting on p. 188); they'll help you get started.

DO I NEED TO FERTILIZE MY GARDEN REGULARLY?

This depends on what type of garden or plants you want to include. If you want a maintenance-free space, focus on plants that are easy to grow, tolerate drought, require little pruning, and deter weeds and pests. However, if you choose plants that require specific soil conditions, you might have to add amendments, especially when you're getting the plants established.

HOW MUCH CAN I GROW IN CONTAINERS?

You can grow your entire garden in pots and other containers. So even if you have a small space, such as a deck, patio, or balcony, don't worry. You still have lots of options. Choose plants that will do well under your conditions. Stock up on pots and other containers. See if you can squeeze in a small raised bed. Try vertical gardening, which can help you raise a lot in a tiny area. Many other people are dealing with this challenge and they'll share useful tips online, at your garden center, and in various publications. With good planning, you can grow more than you thought possible.

SHOULD I REMOVE SPENT PLANTS IN THE FALL?

It's tempting to clean up your garden as the plants start to wither and turn brown. However, if you want to attract as much wildlife as possible, consider leaving them up year-round. You can still do a little tidying, but try to wait to remove most of the previous year's plant matter until the start of the next growing season. By doing this, you'll offer food, cover, and shelter for wildlife.

WHAT IF IT'S CHALLENGING TO WATER REGULARLY?

Many gardeners have a hard time watering their garden regularly. They might just forget, be unable to irrigate while they're on vacation, or be limited by water restrictions. If you think this might be an issue for you, focus on drought-tolerant plants. Fortunately, many native plants are naturally drought tolerant.

PHOTOGRAPHY AND ILLUSTRATION CREDITS

Garden illustrations by Jenna Lechner

Holly Kuchera, pp. 191 (bottom); 181 (bottom)

Howard Cheek, p. 21 (left)

Howard Nevitt, Jr., p. 37

Iebele Hut, p. 161 (right)

Ileana Marcela Bosogea Tudor, pp. 168 (bottom, left), 183 (left)

Iva Villi, p. 107

Ivonne Wierink, p. 111 (right)

James53145, p. 168 (middle, left)

Jan Rozehnal, p. 96 (top, center)

Jane Bettany, p. 162 (left)

Jhogan, p. 179 (bottom)

Joloei, p. 167 (left)

Jorge Salcedo, p. 108 (left)

Jrtmedia, p. 94 (roight)

Julio Salgado, p. 43 (right)

K Quinn Ferris, pp. 5, 138

Karin De Mamiel, p. 129 (center, right)

Katarzyna Mazurowska, p. 112 (left)

Kazakovmaksim, p. 125 (right)

Keith Lejon, p. 45 (bottom, right)

Keith Neu, p. 130 (middle, left)

Kenneth Keifer, p. 176 (bottom)

Kenz Hanson, p. 101 (left)

Kim Nelson, p. 93 (left)

Kondou, p. 129 (bottom, center)

Krzysztof Slusarczyk, p. 130 (bottom, left)

Kyaw Thiha, p. 151

Larry Metayer, p. 152 (right)

Lawsonpix, p. 199 (top)

Le Thuy Do, pp. 199 (bottom); 150 (left)

Leerobin, p. 142 (right)

Les Palenik, p. 188 (top)

Lesia Kapinosova, p. 94 (left)

Lianem, pp. 92; 130 (bottom, right)

Lightpoet, p. 177 (bottom)

Lijuan Guo, p. 61 (left)

Llmckinne, p. 44

Loflo69, p. 158 (left)

Lorraine Swanson, p. 48 (left)

Lthomas57, pp. 130 (top, center), 136 (right)

Luckydoor, p. 88 (left)

Lukich, p. 21 (right)

Lutz Gerken, p. 64 (left)

Marcin Ciesielski/Sylwia Cisek, p. 123 (left)

Maria Dryfhout, pp. 10, 12 (bottom, right), 55, 196 (top)

Marianne Lachance, p. 66 (middle, center)

Marjatta Caján, pp. 117; 166

Mark Herreid, p. 197 (top)

Mark Hryciw, p. 31

Martin Sevcik, p. 64 (right)

Mashiki, p. 194 (bottom)

Matthew Benoit, p. 180 (top)

Maxliv, p. 168 (middle, right)

Melodyanne, p. 23 (right)

Menno67, p. 33 (left)

Mesquite53, p. 75 (bottom, left)

Meunierd, p. 174 (top)

Michael Mill, p. 20 (left)

Mihail Ivanov, pp. 186 (top, right); 129 (top, right)

Mike Nettleship, p. 116

Miroslav Hlavko, p. 167 (right)

Mkos83, p. 51

Motorolka, p. 149 (left)

Mrehssani, p. 130 (bottom, center)

Nadmak2010, p. 60

Narith Thongphasuk, p. 209

Nataliia Vyshneva, p. 161 (left)

Nikita Tiunov, p. 164 (right)

Nikolai Kurzenko, p. 129 (top, left)

Norman Bateman, p. 147

Norman Chan, pp. 119, 201 (top)

Oleksandr Panchenko, p. 65

Onepony, pp. 47 (right); 63 (right); 66 (middle, right)

Oseland, p. 96 (bottom, right)

Parthkumar Bhatt, p. 96 (bottom, left)

Pasqueflower, p. 154 (right)

Passion4Nature, p. 207 (top)

Paul Lemke, pp. 40; 136 (left)

Paul Reeves, pp. 102 (right); 139 (left); 174 (bottom)

Paul Sparks, p. 28 (left)

Paveerisa Sarutwattananont, p. 84 (left)

Pavel Cheiko, p. 129 (bottom, left)

Peregrine, p. 200 (bottom)

Petar Kremenarov, p. 27 (left)

Photozirka, p. 87 (right)

Pimmimemom, p. 78 (left)

Pixelarchitect, pp. 66 (top, left), 76

Pozitivstudija, p. 85

Pp1, p. 144 (left)

Prakong Lim, p. 157 (right)

Pstedrak, p. 153 (right)

Rachel Hopper, p. 103

Randall Runtsch, p. 18 (right)

Rbiedermann, p. 193 (top)

René Pirker, p. 168 (middle, center)

Revensis, p. 93 (right)

Ridjin, p. 192 (top)

Rinus Baak, pp. 12 (top, right); 28 (right); 45 (top, left; top, right); 72; 75 (top, right); 95

Rob Lumen Captum, p. 126

Robert Hambley, pp. 35; 42

Ruud Morijn, p. 66 (bottom, center)

Samsam62, p. 154 (left)

Sandyprints, p. 150 (right)

Sarah Robson, p. 123 (right)

Saurabh13, p. 36 (right)

Seanjeeves, p. 130 (middle, center)

Seksuwat, p. 12 (middle, right)

Seramo, p. 160

Serban Enache, p. 120 (right)

Sergey Kohl, p. 83 (right)

Silvia Ganora, p. 127

Sjankauskas, p. 66 (bottom, left)

Skorpionik00, p. 159

Stefan Malloch, p. 38 (left)

Stephanie Nicole Castle Brookus, p. 52

Steve Byland, pp. 23 (left); 27 (right); 32; 33 (right); 35 (right); 45 (middle, left); 66 (bottom, right); 75 (bottom, right); 144 (right); 178 (top)

Stevebrigman, p. 30 (left)

Stubblefieldphoto, p. 20 (right)

Sue Feldberg, p. 22

Sylwia Szmulewicz Pączkowska, p. 129 (middle, right)

Tamara Kulikova, p. 189 (middle)

Tatyana Azarova, p. 96 (top, right)

Tatyanaego, p. 50 (right)

Teekaygee, p. 39

Thomas Woodruff, p. 202 (bottom)

Tim Heusinger Von Waldegge, p. 102 (left)

Vaivirga, pp. 62 (left); 111 (left)

Valerii Maksimov, p. 212

Veronika Viskova, p. 121 (right)

Victor Savushkin, p. 50 (left)

Viorel Dudau, p. 115 (left)

Volga1971, p. 122

Wayne Mckown, p. 175 (top)

Weldon Schloneger , p. 59 (right)

Wildphotos, p. 45 (bottom, center)

William Perry, p. 180 (bottom)

Zerenz, p. 158 (right)

Zestmarina, p. 179 (top)

Zhanghaobeibei, pp. 114; 201 (bottom)

Zo Moussaoui, p. 129 (middle, center)

SHUTTERSTOCK

Agnieszka Bacal, p. 2

Erik Karets, p. 101 (right)

FamStudio, p. 201 (middle)

Fedotova Olga, p. 195 (top)

Uryupina Nadezhda, p. 215

Wirestock Creators, p. 80 (left)

FLICKR

Jordi Segers/Canadian Wildlife Health Center, p. 173 (bottom)

Kelly Colgan Azar, p. 168 (bottom, center)

INDEX

TINA GREGORY

STACY TORNIO is the author of more than fifteen books for families and kids, including *The National Parks Scavenger Hunt*, *101 Outdoor Adventures to Have Before You Grow Up*, and *The Kids' Outdoor Adventure Book*, the latter two recipients of National Outdoor Book Awards. She is a former editor of *Birds & Blooms* magazine and currently runs the website BeAGoodHuman.co.